rooted
(IN)

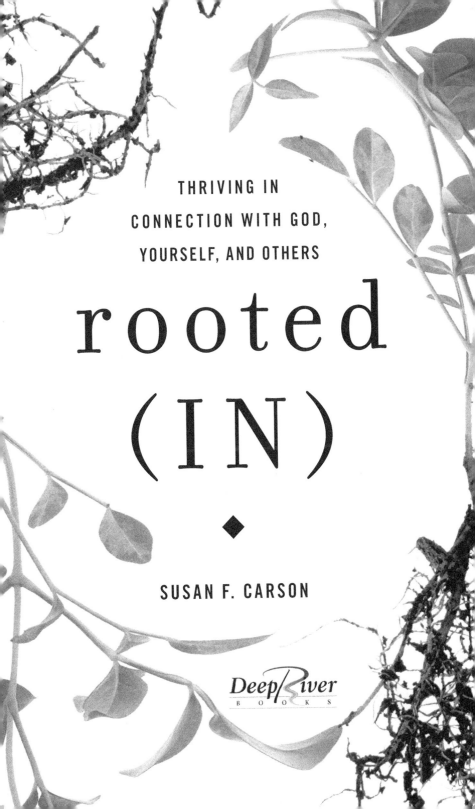

THRIVING IN
CONNECTION WITH GOD,
YOURSELF, AND OTHERS

rooted
(IN)

◆

SUSAN F. CARSON

Deep River
B O O K S

ISBN – 13: 9781632695086
Library of Congress: 2019941303

Printed in the USA
2019—First Edition

28 27 26 25 24 23 22 21 20 19   10 9 8 7 6 5 4 3 2 1

Cover design: Connie Gabbert
Interior design: Robin Black, Inspirio Design

WHAT LEADERS ARE SAYING ABOUT ROOTED (IN): THRIVING IN CONNECTION WITH GOD, YOURSELF, AND OTHERS

"Susan has written such an accessible guide to spiritual growth and transformation. Personal, practical, and authentic in style, this book will help you go to the next level in your relationship with God and your enjoyment of life in Him."

Chuck Mingo
Teaching Pastor and Oakley Community Pastor, Crossroads Church

"Susan has a beautiful way of offering truth while being vulnerable. She dives deep into God's truth on how shame and lies distort who God made us to be. This is a story of leaving shame behind and stepping into the deepest kind of love, firmly rooted in truth, and connected with God. What a gift to the faith community she has given us!"

Beth Guckenberger
Co-Executive Director, Back2Back Ministries; speaker and author of
Start with Amen: How I Learned to Surrender by Keeping the End in Mind

"Susan Carson shapes a space for freedom and transformation. She's learned it from years in ministry—drawing on ancient practices, scriptural wisdom, and personal experience—and now makes that space available in this book. If you will enter *IN* to this gracious, imaginative, hopeful space, you may just find yourself in a new place with God."

Mandy Smith
Pastor, University Christian Church; author, *The Vulnerable Pastor*

"In *Rooted (IN): Thriving in Connection with God, Yourself, and Others*, Susan Carson shows you practical ways to heal your hidden brokenness and unhealthy behaviors by recognizing the root. This book equips you to live fully, joyfully, and lovingly, with healing and wholeness in Jesus Christ. I am excited that Susan has written this book, including her personal healing journey. It will empower you and stir your heart to draw closer to Jesus by the Holy Spirit. If you want to grow in with love God, yourself, and others, you will love this book!"

Rev. Dr. SueLee Jin
Pastor, Anderson Hills United Methodist Church; faculty mentor,
United Theological Seminary (Randy Clark Scholars Focus Group)

"With wit and candor, Susan Carson masterfully weaves story and Scripture and sages' quotes into this inspiring book. Clearly she knows what it means to live deeply rooted in the love of God—a relationship forged through her own healing journey with Jesus and the remarkable friendship that has ensued. No reader will be untouched or left doubting that Jesus is still very much among us, working miracles in the midst of life's most confounding challenges!"

Beth A. Booram
Co-founder and Director, Fall Creek Abbey;
spiritual director; author, *Starting Something New*, and
coauthor with husband David, *When Faith Becomes Sight*

"In the current climate of fragmentation in almost every arena of life—God, ourselves, others and the world around us—Susan sets forth a strong and winsome image of being rooted in God's love in the whole of our stories. The book is an invitation to engage in more than simply believing God loves you . . . but to actually engage in practices like silence and solitude. This book gives you the principles and prayerful practices that a person needs to stop being stuck and start living a life marked by joy, meaning, and abundance. She is speaking God's desire for each of us to be who we really are in Him. If you have not yet embarked on this journey of being who you really are, or gotten stalled along the way, this book will guide you well."

Sibyl Towner
Coauthor, *Listen to My Life*; cofounder, OneLifeMaps.com; and codirector, The Springs Retreat Center, Oldenburg, Indiana

"With disarming vulnerability, Susan Carson deftly balances her own story and experiences with Scripture and time-tested practices. This is not the work of a theoretician, but a fellow sojourner and practitioner offering practical help and hope. In our hurried, frantic culture, this deeply life-affirming book is much needed cool water for thirsty souls, gently reminding readers of the Father's love and the much richer life He offers."

Dave Workman
President, Elemental Churches; author, *Elemental Leaders: Four Essentials Every Leader Needs . . . and Every Church Must Have* and *The Outward-Focused Life: Becoming a Servant in a Serve-Me World*

"A thoughtful book about life with God that is both informative and provocative, written with heart and soul that is relevant and relatable. I appreciate the inclusion of practical exercises within the book that offer daily application for going deeper in the spiritual journey."

Dr. Candyce Roberts
Author, *Help for the Fractured Soul* and *Sharing a Table: Knowing the Love Of God in Community*

"Susan is offering the authentic pathway she used to find the deep joy and contentment that we all seek. She tenaciously pursued the real God and found him to be trustworthy and crazy in love with her. You'll be inspired, challenged, encouraged and thankful for Susan's vulnerability, sense of humor, practical wisdom and doable suggestions for finding spiritual wholeness void of performance-based living. She'll lead you to know and experience how God is crazy in love with you, too!"

Dr. Marcia Ball
Co-founder and Executive Director, Kerus Global Education;
co-author, *It Takes Courage: Promoting Character and Healthy Life Choices*

"Through her story, Susan Carson opens readers to their own stories, helping them connect with their true identity as ones fully loved by God. We cannot fully love ourselves or others without first receiving the love of a Father. I recommend this book to anyone wanting to grow in the deep parts of their journey with God. The invitation is open to all, no matter where you are in your journey. There's always more to discover. His love is never ending and His invitation is always steady."

Kristan Dooley
Discipleship Pastor, Anthem House Church; Director, Renewal Women;
author, *Bigger: Rebuilding the Broken*

To Virginia

For your journey of becoming who you already are

◆

contents

◆

The Journey (IN) and Why Roots Matter

*The farther the outward journey takes you,
the deeper the inner journey must be. Only when your roots
are deep can your fruits be abundant.*
—HENRI NOUWEN[1]

*The root of Christian love is not the will to love, but the faith that one is
loved. The faith that one is loved by God.*
—THOMAS MERTON[2]

WE ARE ALL ON A JOURNEY of becoming who we already are. We are already fully loved, created with intention to live with joy and significance. To thrive in spirit, soul, and body. To live deeply connected with God, with our true selves, and with others.

But something is in the way.

I've experienced it, too. Shame, pain, and disappointments leave you isolated and separated from God, yourself, and others. You end up going through life outside yourself, striving for acceptance, longing for love and grace.

Rooted (IN) is a journey out of shame into love. The spiritual paths and practices in this book open the way to living rooted and grounded in the healing, restoring love of Christ. Over decades and as director of Roots&Branches Network, I've had the honor of praying with hundreds of people, helping them do the same. And I've learned the only way out of our shame and pain is (IN).

Rooted (IN) gives you the principles and prayerful practices you need to stop being stuck and start living a life full of joy and meaning with your tribe. Just as the word IN is held within parentheses throughout this book, you are surrounded and held by the unflinching, unchanging love of God. And it is this (IN) that makes all the difference.

WHAT'S AHEAD

In Part One, we'll explore foundational principles for a life rooted (IN) and remaining (IN) the love of God. In Parts Two and Three, we'll explore spiritual practices for living more deeply rooted (IN) loving connection with God, with ourselves, and with our world. In each chapter of this book, we'll experience new ways to connect, to put down roots deep and wide in grace that nourishes and heals the soul. Each chapter represents a principle and practice that will help you live more rooted. Listening in the quiet. Listening to God, to yourself, to others. Silence. Solitude. Sacraments. Grace. Truth. Healing. Prayer. Ancient and modern paths and practices that bring life.

To get the most out of this book, I encourage you to do three things:

1. Read the book and understand the journey (IN). Do this with yourself or with a few friends.
2. Do the "Deeper (IN)" experiences at the end of each chapter.
3. Pick a few new practices you'll engage in regularly.

You are made to live rooted and grounded in a lasting experience of God's love. With new practices, you'll learn to remove roots blocking and breaking this connection—roots that have gone down in places of pain and disappointment, carrying toxins of doubt, fear, and judgment to body, soul, and spirit. You'll learn how to replace old, unhealthy roots with new roots connected in love and truth. And you'll learn to live more present to God, to your own heart, and to others.

All that is gold does not glitter,
Not all those who wander are lost;
The old that is strong does not wither,
Deep roots are not reached by the frost.
From the ashes a fire shall be woken,
A light from the shadows shall spring;
Renewed shall be blade that was broken,
The crownless again shall be king.

—J.R.R. Tolkien[3]

The root is certainly a more decisive factor than what is growing above ground. After all, it is the root that looks after the survival of an organism. It is the root that has withstood severe changes in climatic conditions. And it is the root that has regrown trunks time and time again. It is in the roots that centuries of experience are stored, and it is this experience that has allowed the trees survival to the present day.

—Peter Wohlleben, *The Hidden Life of Trees*[1]

PART ONE

◆

LIVING ROOTED
IN LOVE

CHAPTER 1

◆

Deeper (IN)

*Love is like a tree: it grows by itself, roots itself deeply
in our being and continues to flourish over a heart in ruin.
The inexplicable fact is that the blinder it is, the more tenacious it is.
It is never stronger than when it is completely unreasonable.*
—VICTOR HUGO[1]

I REMEMBER BEING ALONE. A lot. Not that my parents weren't there; they were. But what I feel as I journey through memories is almost nothing. A vacuum. Emptiness of substance, emotionally, spiritually. And I see myself alone. Playing alone. In my room, mostly. Or in the family room with the '60s red shag carpet. My mother somewhere in the house reading. My father gone, at work. Or angry. Mostly, I remember being alone.

Some of my first memories are of my best friend Sheila, who lived right across the street, and several other friends who lived just houses away. Our neighborhood felt like one big playground. Our mothers sent us outside in the morning, and we played together all day long—first in my backyard, then in all the others. It was magical. It felt safe. I belonged. Until we moved.

My father's anger and inability to stay very long in any job meant we moved several times as I was growing up. At the end of second grade, we moved from Cincinnati to Lexington, Kentucky. I still remember looking out the back window of the car as we pulled away, waving to Sheila and sobbing. My sense of security was slipping away with each mile.

Lexington was hard. Then McAllen, Texas, for seventh grade was harder. On the border of Mexico. Culture shock. Then North Webster, Indiana, for eighth grade and high school. A tiny, one-stop-light lake town. Another kind of culture shock. Each move was harder. And as an introvert—an extreme, please-don't-make-me-talk kind of introvert—I had more and more trouble connecting in life. Friendships were lost with each move. I was lost more and more with each move.

A disconnected teenager will do almost anything to find affinity and affirmation. It's a bit of a cliché. Troubled teen makes bad choices. That was me. Without any emotional or spiritual grounding, without any sense of myself, I was desperate to find the people who would provide that. The summer before my senior year of high school, I decided I would do whatever it took to be popular, to finally fit in, belong. I wouldn't compromise my grades, because my grades were my identity. But I would compromise myself in every other way. In our school, the popular crowd was smart—honor-society smart. And the popular crowd partied hard. Drinking. Drugs. They were very happy to bring me in and took great joy in my corruption. I was finally in. And I was more alone than ever. Darkness and depression swallowed me whole.

Word that I was out of control, struggling, reached three teachers. These three ate lunch together every day in an office with doors open, open to students who wanted to talk. Two of these teachers knew Jesus. And one was my physics teacher. One day during a lab, Mr. Kitson called me into his office, closed the door, and started talking about Jesus. I wasn't raised in church. I knew next to nothing about Jesus—except that Christmas and Easter had something to do with him. I didn't have a grid for anything he was saying. I might as well have been listening to Charlie Brown's teacher: "Wha wha wha wha wha, Jesus, wha wha wha." But what I knew when I returned to my lab was something about Jesus was important, and someone cared enough about me to throw me a lifeline.

A few weeks later, as I stood in our kitchen holding a knife to my wrist, I had a rare moment of clarity. I could end it now. Or I could try the God thing. Since I had nothing to lose and the rest of my life to gain, it seemed like giving Jesus a shot was a good idea. The next day I asked Mr. Kitson what I should do. He pointed me to a church within walking distance of my house, filled with people who loved Jesus, and he said I should get a Bible and read the book of John. I immediately did both.

The people at that little church embraced me, and the youth group took me in. I started reading the book of John and I could not stop. The stories were alive to me, and it was all such amazingly good news. How come no one had ever told me about this Jesus? News this good, a story this good, everyone should know. When I finished John, I kept reading, making my way through the New Testament. A few months later I was about midway through the book of Romans when my youth pastor called the question: Was there any reason I wasn't ready to follow Jesus? All the reasons not to were gone.

We knelt together at the altar rail of the little church. Just the two of us. And I prayed. I told Jesus I'd messed things up. I needed him. I needed forgiveness. And I would follow him. I gave everything to him that day. And a world sideways and gray turned suddenly upright and full color. When I opened my eyes, everything looked different—which I know sounds weird, but it really did. Like going from an old black-and-white TV to HD color. And I felt different. Joy came in.

So much changed when I gave my life to Jesus. But the depression of my childhood still hung like a shadow around me. Six weeks later I began my freshman year at Vanderbilt University, knowing little about my new faith and even less about myself. I began to learn more about Jesus and what it meant to follow him. I learned about Bible study tools, Scripture memorization, serving, prayer, and many good things that formed a foundation of faith in my life. My head learned a lot about Jesus, and I loved him more than ever. But my heart was disconnected from so much of what I was learning, unable to experience the truth of his love for me. I worked hard to do all the right things, because that's what a perfectionistic performer does. And it helped for a while. And then it didn't. At the core, I was still alone.

I realized gradually, through years of counseling and healing prayer, that I had no sense of self. No sense of myself at all. I was afraid that if you peeled back all the layers of me, there was nothing at the core. Nothing of substance. That after more than twenty years on this planet, I really didn't exist. It seems crazy, but there it is: The part that is uniquely me, my spirit, had never been seen, recognized, blessed, connected. The aloneness I'd experienced as a child and the lies that came with it had embedded in my soul. I struggled for years with depression as I walked into greater measures of healing.

I am still walking. Still healing. Still becoming more fully who I've been all along.

ROOTS MATTER

For trees and everything that grows from the ground, roots are the life source. And since we are made from the dust of a garden, the same is true for us. Nourishment for our soul—our mind, will, and emotions—comes through the roots. What we are rooted (IN), what we are connected to and through, matters.

As an only child growing up in many ways emotionally and spiritually disconnected, I put down a very big root in isolation. My identity drew (in part) from this root of isolation, nourishing the message that I was alone, unloved, unchosen. My true self withered, and false self flourished, as my identity—my sense of self—grew twisted, misshapen by lies.

At the same time isolation was rooting in my life, my grandparents gave me a gift of belonging. They purchased a farm in Wilmington, Ohio when my grandfather retired, with the intention of creating a special place for their grandchildren. For me, that place was magical. It was the constant in the midst of all our moves. It was long days with my cousins. Coffee cans filled with fireflies. Barn cats. Tractor rides. Pond frogs. A secret clubhouse (OK, maybe not so secret) in the shed. In this place, I also put down a very big root. My identity drew (in part) from this root, nourishing the message that I belonged. That I was not alone. That I had a place. The gift of the farm and my time there nourished my true self in a way that sustained and formed me, in spite of the lies.

That place, the farm, remains in me. Those memories and all that's embedded in them, the belonging and safety, are life to me. Every time I see fireflies or Queen Anne's lace, it all comes back. In the summer we'd pick these beautiful lacey white flowers and put them in empty jelly jars filled with water and drops of food coloring. Then we'd watch as the flowers slowly began to change colors. The stems of the flowers drawing the blue or red or purple up into the lace. Just as those flowers were changed by color they drew from the water, I was changed by the stability I drew from the farm.

ABOUT A TREE

Our unique stories shape us, for better and worse. Memories embedded in our souls (neuroscience would tell us exactly where in our brains) hold emotions connected with our beliefs about what we experienced (or didn't experience). A child who remembers being alone holds sadness and the belief she is unwanted, unchosen. A child who remembers being connected holds stability and the belief she has a place. It's all in there together, with a whole lot more. And it all forms the soil we draw from, the places we are rooted. We are all a very mixed bag of nuts—the good and bad together.

So maybe, since we've been talking about roots, it's not a surprise that our story begins with a tree. In a garden. A tree that held the fruit of the knowledge of good and bad together. In the garden, Eve and Adam walked and talked in the open with God. Nothing hidden. Nothing covered. They lived completely connected with the God who'd made them for himself and for each other, connected with one another as equal partners made together to contain the fullness of God's goodness. They enjoyed the beauty of the garden and the fruit of all the trees, save one. They were one with God. One flesh together. And they felt no shame, no sense they had anything to hide.

And then they ate. You probably know the story. Eve and Adam believed the lie told by the serpent that they needed something more—that who they were, what they had, was not enough. (Does that lie sound familiar at all to you?) They ate the fruit because it looked lovely and promised wisdom, a greater knowing . . . or so said the serpent. But these two were made only for the good, and suddenly they felt something God never intended. Good and evil together. And with that evil came shame. They covered up. And we still do the same thing today.

When Adam and Eve heard the sound of God walking in the garden, they hid. And perfect union, unbroken connection, was shattered in the silence. "I heard you in the garden," Adam says, "and I was afraid because I was naked; so I hid."[2] The knowing brings shame, and the shame brings fear. And all work together to separate. Adam and Eve no longer felt safe with God. Nor with each other. And with that, our shared journey through pain, out of shame and fear, our journey back to connection, begins.

ROOTED CONNECTION THAT HEALS

So how do we deal with the shame and the fear and all the places we see the fruit of bentness and brokenness in our lives? Religion's answer is focused on outward behavior—a try-harder kind of legalism. Read more, serve more, pray more, repent more. People look good on the outside, but they're dying on the inside. They hide their true selves in shame. The message is that who you are is not OK—in fact, your heart is bad and you are bad.

But the good news is so much better than this. (IN) Christ, connection is restored. As our shame is unearthed, we live more and more rooted in love, becoming more and more who we already are. Created in his image. Fully known. Fully loved. This journey of becoming begins with the simple wanting and asking. It begins with a prayer:

> I pray that out of his glorious riches he may strengthen you with power through his Spirit in your inner being, so that Christ may dwell in your hearts through faith. And I pray that you, being rooted and established in love, may have power, together with all the Lord's holy people, to grasp how wide and long and high and deep is the love of Christ, and to know this love that surpasses knowledge—that you may be filled to the measure of all the fullness of God.[3]

Stop for a minute. Read this passage again slowly. Out loud. As a prayer. Breathe it in. Breathe it out. Rootedness is the place of fullness, the fullness of God in us. God's love permeating us, forming us, nourishing us. In this place, this rooted and grounded place, we know the unknowable. We know, not in a heady, cerebral, factoid, I-just-listened-to-a-great-podcast kind of way. We know in the real, experiential, feel-it-in-my-core kind of way. We know and live from the vastness of God's strong love for us. This is rooted living.

This is my favorite prayer in the Bible. I pray this for myself and for others a lot because I don't know—we don't know—the size of God's love for us. We have no idea. (Or maybe you do. In which case I'd like to meet you and buy you lunch and hear all about that, because I have a whole bunch of questions for you.) And what I do know I forget. All the time.

We are meant to live rooted and grounded in the love of God. The love expressed to us in Christ, in creation, in our life and breath, in every good gift. We are meant to live with the very person who is God's love expressed, the Spirit of Jesus, dwelling in us. With this Spirit of love, joy, peace, patience, kindness, goodness filling us, seeping out of our pores. We are meant to live with the power that comes as we know this love, the huge expanse of it. Wider, deeper, thicker than the ocean. This fullness, this love that surpasses knowledge, filling us with the very fullness of God. (Holy cow.)

Living rooted in this—knowing this deeply, experientially, not just in my head, but in my heart—changes everything. It changes me. It changes my relationships with others. It changes my relationship with God. This love is the beginning and end of everything. We can only be rightly connected with God, ourselves, and others to the extent that our roots go deep and deeper still in love.

Social researcher and author Dr. Brené Brown defines connection as "the energy that exists between people when they feel seen, heard, and valued; when they can give and receive without judgment; and when they derive sustenance and strength from the relationship."[4] Brilliant. And I think this is also true between people and God. When we experience being seen, heard, and valued by God. When we receive from God without judgment. And when we derive strength and sustenance from God. This is when healing happens. And this sounds a lot like love, doesn't it? It's the atmosphere in which love takes root and grows. Masks come off. We uncover and come out from hiding. And we become a little more whole.

This kind of connection—the "I see and know you, I am here for you, I accept and value you" kind of bond—comes with a knowing that is experienced. It's not a thought or an idea. It's a reality we are meant to feel deeply because we've known the presence of God with us, in us. The fullness of all of God's love crashing in on us and spilling out of us. This kind of connection nourishes the soil of our souls, soil ready to receive the seeds that bear the crop of joy. In the words of Trappist monk and writer Thomas Merton:

> Every moment and every event of every man's life on earth plants something in his soul. For just as the wind carries thousands of winged seeds, so each moment brings with it germs of spiritual vitality that come to rest imperceptibly in the minds and wills of men. Most of these unnumbered seeds perish and are lost, because men are not prepared to receive them: for such seeds as these cannot spring up anywhere except in the good soil of freedom, spontaneity, and love.[5]

REMOVING TO RESTORE

Roots go down in our lives in the moments when deep agreement is made with a belief (true or false) about ourselves, God, and/or others. This happens in childhood. In adolescence. It may even happen today over lunch. Things happen to us and around us, and we make decisions about what these things mean. A parent says something in anger. An abuser violates. A friend or partner abandons. A teacher gives a grade. A parent encourages. A friend or partner gives unconditional love. We have a sense of place and constancy. We lose a sense of place and constancy. We are shamed. We are blessed. We are bullied. And through it all, we make judgments, both good and bad, about ourselves, others, even about God, based on our perceptions of what we've experienced. When we agree with these judgments, we put down roots in good soil and in bad; and these judgments, the true and the false together, nourish and shape our lives.

Soon after I was born, my mom had a series of miscarriages. I don't have any cognitive memories of these first years of my life; but at some point I became aware that these miscarriages had happened, and I made some decisions, from my child perspective, about what that meant about me. I decided these miscarriages meant, since my parents wanted more children, I wasn't enough for them, and it was my responsibility to make up for all those children. I had to be all those children for my mom and dad.

Sounds crazy, right? That a child would draw and live from conclusions like this. But as children, we perceive and interpret as children, internalizing messages that the adults and authorities in our lives may have never intended. My parents never said this to me. I don't think they ever intentionally acted in a way that would have led me to this conclusion. But as a child, I observed and decided. I put down a root, picked up a huge burden, and the lie of "not enough" was planted in my soul soil. From this root came the fruits of performance and perfectionism, and behaviors driven by the need to be more and other than I was created to be.

In the same way, roots go down when we are violated. When we experience pain and trauma. When we experience life, blessing, and encouragement. Roots go down in places that bring death and make our souls and bodies sick. Roots go down in places that bring health and life to our spirit, soul, and body.

When we are rooted in the false, we live from unhealthy beliefs that lead to unhealthy emotions and behaviors. When we are rooted in the true, we thrive. Who and what we are connected to, what we are rooted in, matters. Life and health are in the roots. It's true for trees. It's true for us.

THE FRUIT WILL LEAD YOU TO THE ROOT

Where do you feel stuck in your life? What patterns and behaviors keep repeating, no matter how hard you to try to break them? And I mean, you've tried. Counseling. Dieting. New disciplines. More prayer. Support groups. Meditation and mantras. You're still stuck. And that big overreaction yesterday—where did that come from? The nice lady in the car in front of you is driving a little too slowly. You are, after all, in a hurry for something very important. And you're saying, maybe screaming, not very nice things about her. Why are you so angry?

Why do you seem to attract only toxic relationships? Why are you continually worried about the future? Why can you just not seem to break that habit? The unwanted, unhealthy fruit in your life, the behaviors and beliefs you desperately want to change, is a signpost. An invitation. It invites you to look deeper. To find a place where you're living rooted in something that's not bringing life. That angry overreaction in traffic may point to something deeper. Perhaps a place you're rooted in anger, still angry about something that happened yesterday or last month or when you were five. Unhealthy patterns in relationships, addictive behaviors, coping mechanisms, depression, phobias . . . the fruit you see in your life will lead you to the root. And when you find the root, the real reason you've been so stuck—and it's almost never what you think—you can make the exchange. False for true. Bad soil for good.

Roots and trees and lives and relationships thrive when they are planted in good soil. Jesus shared this timeless principle in a parable:

> A farmer went out to sow his seed. As he was scattering the seed, some fell along the path, and the birds came and ate it up. Some fell on rocky places, where it did not have much soil. It sprang up quickly, because the soil was shallow. But when the sun came up, the plants were scorched, and they withered because they had no root. Other seed fell among thorns, which grew up and choked the plants. Still other seed fell on good soil, where it produced a crop—a hundred, sixty or thirty times what was sown. Whoever has ears, let them hear.[6]

Seeds need enough of the right soil, good soil, to grow and produce fruit. The worries and troubles and hardships of life work to steal and choke and scorch the life right out of you. But in good soil, good seeds put down roots that sustain life. Jesus says the good soil refers to someone who hears the word and understands it. Someone who hears and believes and begins to live in the truth that God is here with me, (IN) me, to redeem and restore in love. Where our soul soil is good, the truth about God, us, and others takes root to produce good fruit. Where our soul soil is still tainted by lies about God, us, and others, we remain unable to sustain life. It's what we're rooted in that determines whether we wither or thrive.

THE OTHER TREE

Turns out, it all comes back to a tree again. The tree of life was the other tree in the garden at the very beginning. It's been here. It's been God's intention and invitation all along.

> Then the angel showed me the river of life, as clear as crystal, flowing from the throne of God and of the Lamb, down the middle of the great street of the city. On each side of the river stood the tree of life, bearing the twelve crops of fruit, yielding its fruit every month. And the leaves of the tree are for the healing of the nations.[7]

The fruit of this tree is available to us now, today. Fruitfulness coming again and again in our lives, over and over, as we are restored. And not just us. Did you notice? It's a healing in community. A healing of the nations. God making us one again, connected in love.

So how? you ask. How do I find the roots and remove them? How do I cultivate the soil of my soul? How do I exchange the fruit of the one tree for the other? That's what the rest of this book is about. So keep reading. Keep journeying. Love is waiting.

DEEPER (IN)

Each chapter will end with a spiritual practice or two to help you connect with the principles. These experiences will help concepts migrate the long distance from your head to your heart, to help you experience what we're talking about. You might find a journal helpful for writing your responses and reflections. Let's dive (IN).

Breath Prayer

Let's look again at the prayer in Ephesians 3:16–19:

> I pray that out of his glorious riches he may strengthen you with power through his Spirit in your inner being, so that Christ may dwell in your hearts through faith. And I pray that you, being rooted and established in love, may have power, together with all the Lord's holy people, to grasp how wide and long and high and deep is the love of Christ, and to know this love that surpasses knowledge— that you may be filled to the measure of all the fullness of God.

Now make this prayer personal by turning it into a breath prayer. A breath prayer is a short, simple prayer of just a few words prayed with an inhale and an exhale. Three or four words on the inhale. Three of four words on the exhale. Slow and steady.

Write your own breath prayer from Ephesians 3. Just six or eight words that reflect your desire for deep connection. As you craft it, practice it to be sure it feels unforced and unhurried. This week, pray your breath prayer throughout each day. If it still isn't feeling right, keep changing it until you land on your unique prayer. Continue to breathe this prayer in and out throughout your journey (IN). This simple prayer will open the way for the transformation ahead.

Journeying with a Few Friends

If you decide to take the journey (IN) with a small group, these three things will be helpful:

1. Read about creating a rooted community (page 223) together. Commit as a group to creating a noise-free, shame-free, formula-free space for one another.

2. Come prepared to share what you learned or experienced through the Deeper (IN) activities. The more honestly and authentically you share, the deeper your group will go together.

3. Use these discussion questions as guides as you process each chapter together:
   - What ideas or concepts did you find most helpful?
   - What questions came to mind as you read?
   - What stories from your own life came to mind as you read?
   - How do the concepts from this chapter apply to your life today?

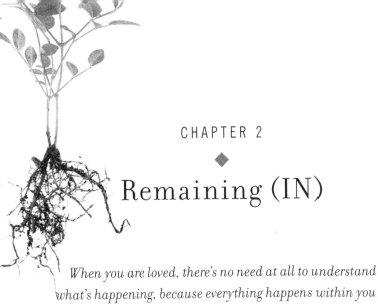

CHAPTER 2

◆

Remaining (IN)

When you are loved, there's no need at all to understand
what's happening, because everything happens within you ...
—PAULO COELHO[1]

"YOU'RE A MESS."

I was working late with my boss who had also become a friend. Really late. Which wasn't unusual in this dysfunctional little marketing research firm. We'd often work past midnight to meet crazy deadlines. Since it was my first job out of college, I assumed this was normal. As we worked, I began to share things from my life. Honestly, I don't remember what. But I do remember being upset and crying.

My boss had experienced this with me before, and this time her response was less empathetic. In fact, it felt harsh. "You're a mess. You need to get some help." Thank you very much, I thought. And ouch. And how dare you. And then, hmm, maybe she's right. Maybe there's another way to live. One without this familiar, pervasive sense of being alone, unloved, unchosen, not enough. Constantly striving to meet an unmeetable standard of perfection. Always feeling like I'm falling short.

The church I attended at that time had a counselor on staff, so I made an appointment to see him. In one of the initial sessions, he pointed to a whiteboard on the wall in his office. "Draw the home you grew up in and place your family members in the picture," he said.

I stared at him blankly, then defiantly. My usually compliant, pleasing self was having none of this. I did not grow up in a single home, so how could I know which one to draw? He suggested I pick the one that felt most representative. This seemed ridiculous and strangely terrifying to me. I kept staring at him, and I told him in no uncertain terms I did not want to do this. I refused. And I felt shocked inside even as I did it. He didn't waver as he placed the pen in my hand. Draw the house. Whatever happened to "please"?

I walked to the board and drew the condo I had most recently lived in with my parents. (Notice any lack of rootedness here?) Then I placed myself upstairs in my bedroom. I placed my mom and dad downstairs in their recliners in front of the TV in the family room. And I stood back. There it was clearly before me. My entire disconnected life. Me alone. I was shaking. It was as if the curtain had been suddenly pulled back and light was pouring in on my life. It felt naked and raw and terrible. But in the light, the unhealthy roots are exposed and healing can begin.

In the last few years prior to this, I had been working hard at college to do the right things, believing that studying the Bible, memorizing the Bible, thinking about the Bible would push back the darkness of depression and isolation. I'd been told and taught that this was the way to know God. But it wasn't working because it was all about my work. I needed grace to loosen the soil around the dark roots in my soul, to open space for light and living water and truth that brings freedom. In the place of grace, I've experienced truth, encountered truth, absorbed truth, and put down new roots in truth. Because grace and truth together are not concepts, they are a person who embodies love. They are Jesus. And finding my life (IN) him has made all the difference.

I'm not sure when this shift started to happen inside me, this work of grace. Slowly, subtly, over time, as I've grown in my experience of his love and the practice of his presence, I have become more real. More fully me. It's been the fruit of listening prayer, healing prayer, time with gifted counselors and spiritual directors and trusted community. It's been the fruit of silence and solitude and more healing. Restoration has come and is coming as I've learned to live in more sustained connection—as I've learned to abide.

ABIDING

> I am the true vine, and my Father is the gardener. He cuts off every branch in me that bears no fruit, while every branch that does bear fruit he prunes so that it will be even more fruitful. You are already clean because of the word I have spoken to you. Remain in me, as I also remain in you. No branch can bear fruit by itself; it must remain in the vine. Neither can you bear fruit unless you remain in me.
>
> I am the vine; you are the branches. If you remain in me and I in you, you will bear much fruit; apart from me you can do nothing.[2]

These are some of the last words spoken by Jesus before his death. During their last supper together, Jesus is telling his closest friends what they need to know to continue once he's gone. Remain. Abide. Stay connected. He uses this same word "remain" eleven times in this final discourse. He says it over and over again. It's apparently really important that the disciples get this. That *we* get this. This is where the life comes. You are clean. You have what you need. Now just stay in this place, as I stay in you. The branch is useless, fruitless, dead all by itself. But connected to the vine, it bears fruit. A lot of fruit. Just stay connected.

The disciples needed to know this, by the way, because this good news is surrounded by some not-so-good news. They will be pruned. They will be persecuted. Life will be hard. Jesus is preparing them for what's to come. They will need to know this to survive. We need to know this to survive. Remain. A branch can do nothing on its own. A branch can only survive and thrive if it stays (IN) the vine.

Our transformation, the restoration of our souls, begins and ends in the place of remaining rooted and grounded in love. As an isolated perfectionist, I'd been working hard to do life and faith right. To prove my identity, my worth, in the doing. The word "no" was not in my vocabulary. I was involved in everything. Available to everyone. Absent any sense of worth apart from the doing, I was a prisoner to my need to be needed.

About two years after my encounter with the whiteboard, some more counseling, and my first experiences with healing prayer, a friend at my second job laid a book on my desk. "I just finished this, and I thought it might be helpful to you." (Honest friends who will share honest truth are gold.) The title of the book was *Codependent No More*. I had no idea what it meant to be codependent. But as I read the book, I felt like the author was writing about me. How does she know? It's like she sees me.

Without any sense of self, I was starving for someone, anyone, to validate me. To need me. To choose me. To say or show my worth. To say "no" was to miss the chance to feed my starving self with another. But all the "yes"es of my life left me compromised, tired, and lost. Nothing inside me was grounded in the unconditional love of God. And hungry for this, I was losing myself in the pursuit of a connection with others that was unbounded and unhealthy. Even in the midst of relationship, I still found myself living with the dark, familiar sense of isolation. No place within knew how to connect to receive life. Abiding changed that for me. Because in abiding, I learned it has nothing to do with the doing and everything to do with the being. "Apart from me, you can do nothing."

As the Father has loved me, so have I loved you. Now remain in my love. If you keep my commands, you will remain in my love, just as I have kept my Father's commands

and remain in his love. I have told you this so that my joy may
be in you and that your joy may be complete. My command
is this: Love each other as I have loved you. Greater love has
no one than this: to lay down one's life for one's friends. You
are my friends if you do what I command. I no longer call
you servants, because a servant does not know his master's
business. Instead, I have called you friends, for everything
that I learned from my Father I have made known to you. You
did not choose me, but I chose you and appointed you so that
you might go and bear fruit—fruit that will last—and so that
whatever you ask in my name the Father will give you. This is
my command: Love each other.[3]

I must have read these words from Jesus dozens of times. I knew
what they said. But I didn't know what they meant. I still thought it was
up to me, all the doing to make myself, my life acceptable. I had a long
list of commandments to obey, to organize my life around. But slowly
the grace of God softened the soil of my heart so truth could take root.
Simple, straightforward, uncomplicated truth. We are fruitful in life
as we remain connected with the One who is love. And in us he fulfills
the commandment to love. We receive love. We give love. As friends
of Jesus. Not servants. Friends. Living in intimate, open connection.
Freely sharing. Freely flowing. Asking. Receiving. In organic, relational connection. This is the life we are meant to have in the vine. It
is a life of being.

And when our life is grounded in this place, we thrive.

LIVING IN UNION

Jesus had a fully connected relationship with his Father. He was clear
about it. "I and the Father are one."[4] No identity issues here. He lived
in the Father as the Father lived in him. And as branches placed in
the vine, we too are made one by the Spirit who lives in us.

If you love me, keep my commands. And I will ask the Father, and he will give you another advocate to help you and be with you forever—the Spirit of truth. The world cannot accept him, because it neither sees him nor knows him. But you know him, for he lives with you and will be in you. I will not leave you as orphans; I will come to you. Before long, the world will not see me anymore, but you will see me. Because I live, you also will live. On that day you will realize that I am in my Father, and you are in me, and I am in you. Whoever has my commands and keeps them is the one who loves me. The one who loves me will be loved by my Father, and I too will love them and show myself to them.[5]

Jesus is in the Father. We are in Jesus. Jesus is (IN) us by his Spirit. We are one bundle of (IN)timate connection. United with Father, Son, and Spirit. Like the disciples, we need to know this to survive. Because the world we live in is hostile, broken, hard. The world we live in says work, strive, move, prove. You are not enough. You are alone. God is not to be trusted. You are not to be trusted.

But the words of Jesus call us back. He is in us by his Spirit based on our yes to him, based on grace alone. We live continually refilled, returning, remaining. Recognizing the Spirit of Jesus in us. We live because he lives in us. We love because he loves in us. In the words of South African pastor and author Andrew Murray:

I am in Him. It makes abiding so simple. If I realize clearly as I meditate: Now I am in him, I see at once that there is nothing lacking but my consent to be what He has made me, to remain where He has placed me. I am in Christ: This simple thought, carefully, prayerfully, believingly uttered, removes the fear that there is yet some great attainment to be reached. No, I am in Christ, my blessed Savior. His love has prepared a home for me with himself. When He says, "Abide in My love," His power has undertaken to open the door and to keep me in this home He has prepared for me, if I will but consent. I am in Christ: Now all I need to say is, "Savior, I thank you for this wondrous grace. I consent; I yield myself to your gracious keeping; I do abide in you."[6]

Abiding is all about sustaining union, remaining connected, being present to the presence of God in us and all around us. Being present to our own lives. Being present to others.

It is so, so hard to stop and simply be. Our noisy world works to keep us busy, distracted, worried. The responsibilities of life, marriage, children, work, church all call to us. Our phones light up with texts and our inboxes fill with emails. So much to be attended to. We think it's up to us, to act and to fix. And in the acting and the fixing we miss our lives. Only as we are present to God and to ourselves in the now, in this singular, never-to-be-duplicated moment, do we draw life from the vine.

KNOWING IN UNION

By the time I faced the terrifying whiteboard in the counselor's office, I'd heard lots of sermons. Read a lot of books. Read a lot of the Bible. And I knew that God loved me. Knew intellectually, in my head, that this was true. But I didn't really know it yet at all. Not in my soul, where I could experience the truth and live grounded in it. Knowing in my soul came with abiding, living rooted and remaining in the God who is love.

We only truly know in union, in deep connection with another. Or with ourselves. We know a lot of things in our head. We have a pretty good idea of what we're supposed to believe. But a lot of it, if we're honest, doesn't feel true at all. We only truly know what we've experienced. In the words of author Leanne Payne, "We come to know ultimate reality, not by theological ideas about it, even though these are valid and necessary, but by union with it—by establishing of a personal relationship between God and man."[7]

"Adam knew Eve and she conceived and bore a son." This kind of knowing requires an experience of intimate union. This isn't Adam knowing about Eve. This is Adam deeply knowing and experiencing Eve as the two become one. This is knowing in union. This is knowing that bears fruit and brings forth life. Multiplication, fruitfulness, comes through union.

"On that day you will realize that I am in my Father, and you are in me, and I am in you." The mind, the will, the character, the very Spirit of God dwells in you. And your mind, will, character, spirit, soul, and body live and move in the God who is love.[8]

God is closer than we think. We are connected (IN) a union that can't be broken, because the permanence of the union doesn't depend on our doing. Nothing can separate you from the love of Christ. Not height. Not depth. Not angels. Not demons. Not life nor death nor anything else in all creation.[9] Nothing. But our experience of this union, knowing the fullness of our life in God, rests in a continuing choice to abide, to yield, to trust, to stay connected. Father Richard Rohr says it this way:

> The Apostle Paul does not primarily talk about individuals. He describes something much larger in which we are participating. His most common phrase is "in Christ." Paul uses it 164 times. How we participate in this reality that is larger than our individual lives is precisely to be in Christ. We are saved by standing consciously inside the force field that is Christ—not by getting it right within our private selves.[10]

In this union, within this holy force field, we come to know our true selves as we come to know this Jesus who shows us what it is to live fully human. Our lives begin to reflect the beauty of his life—centered in and motivated by love, carrying compassion and mercy and healing, living in holy union. All of God, the expansive universe of his love, living in us, available to us in the receiving and remaining. Julian of Norwich describes this kind of intimate knowing:

> For we are so preciously loved by God that we cannot even comprehend it. No created being can ever know how much and how sweetly and tenderly God loves them. It is only with the help of his grace that we are able to persevere in spiritual contemplation with endless wonder at his high, surpassing, immeasurable love which our Lord in his goodness has for us. Therefore we may ask from our Lover to have all of him that we desire. For it is our nature to long for him, and it is his nature to long for us. In this life we can never stop loving him.[11]

BECOMING IN UNION

Rooted in love. Remaining in the vine. From this sacred union, we begin the journey of becoming who we already are. In Jesus, all things wrong have been made right. And all things wrong are being made right. We live in the middle, caught between what is already true and not yet realized. The Spirit, God in us, works to catch us up with what's already happened.

Jesus is all things, and I have all things as I am found in him.[12] All things. I just don't fully know that yet. Because this knowing comes in union. And my experience of this union is still a work in progress. The apostle Paul said it this way: "I do not understand what I do. For what I want to do I do not do, but what I hate I do."[13] Sound familiar?

This tension between the now and the not yet feels like a civil war within—and a house divided can't stand, can't remain. The places within, where I still live rooted in pain and shame, don't yet know the love that heals. And this soul soil still bears the fruit of isolation, depression, self-harm, addiction, anxiety, and every dark thing. But with my every "yes" to God, light breaks in with grace and truth to restore union. And I become a little more fully who I already am.

It is this surrender to love that brings peace. As we bring the places within that divide us back into submission to love, civil war ends and peace (*shalom*) is restored. This beautiful word *shalom* comes from a Hebrew root word meaning "wholeness," and it encompasses completeness, soundness, health, welfare, peace, and contentment. Sounds good, right? In *shalom*, fear, doubt, shame lose ground to love, and the battle is won.

RESTORING UNION

The disciples were confused. Jesus was going away. How were they supposed to remain in him? What did he mean? Really good questions, I think. Questions we still ask today. If you're like me, you'd like a formula. Five or seven or ten steps to abiding. Just do these things, and you're all set to live in perfect union with love. But steps and formulas land us right back again in doing—doing the right things to abide. And it's not about our doing at all. Again from Andrew Murray:

> Our doing and working are but the fruit of Christ's work in us. It is where the soul becomes utterly passive, looking and resting on what Christ is to do, that its energies are stirred to their highest activity, and we work most effectively because we know that He works in us. It is as we see in the words "in Me" the mighty energies of love reaching out after us to have us and to hold us, that all the strength of our will is awakened to abide in Him.[14]

Each remaining chapter in this book examines spiritual practices that will help awaken your soul to abide—to remain rooted and grounded in love. These practices, some ancient, some new, are not formulas or steps. They are, instead, ways of opening your mind, will, and heart to the spiritual work of subtraction—removing, pruning the things that hinder and block to make room for love. All you need, all you are, is already yours (IN) Christ. It's time to know more deeply this love that surpasses knowledge that you may be filled to the full measure with the fullness of God.

DEEPER (IN)

(IN) Prayer

These prayers, one ancient, one modern, can help center you each day in the reality of (IN). Each recognizes the reality that Christ is in us as we are in Christ. I wear a bracelet with the first prayer from St. Patrick as a daily reminder.

Both of these prayers are excerpts of longer prayers that you can find online. Pick the one you like best or alternate between the two. Take just a few minutes each day this week to read slowly through one of these prayers (long or short version—your choice). What images come to mind as you pray? Allow the reality of (IN) to expand in your heart and mind as you consider the words. The answers, the strength, the healing, the hope you need today are not out there somewhere. They are already here. Step (IN).

From St. Patrick's Prayer:[15]
Christ with me,
Christ before me,
Christ behind me,
Christ in me,
Christ beneath me,
Christ above me,
Christ on my right,
Christ on my left,
Christ when I lie down,
Christ when I sit down,
Christ when I arise,
Christ in the heart of every man who thinks of me,
Christ in the mouth of everyone who speaks of me,
Christ in every eye that sees me,
Christ in every ear that hears me.
I arise today
Through a mighty strength, the invocation of the Trinity,
Through belief in the Threeness,
Through confession of the Oneness
of the Creator of creation.

From the "Daily Prayer," John Eldredge:[16]
Heavenly Father, thank you for loving me and choosing me before you made the world. You are my true Father— my creator, redeemer, sustainer, and the true end of all things, including my life. I love you, I trust you, I worship you. I give myself over to you, Father, to be one with you as Jesus is one with you. Thank you for proving your love for me by sending Jesus. I receive him and all his life and all his work which you ordained for me. Thank you for including me in Christ, forgiving me my sins, granting me his righteousness, making me complete in him. Thank you for making me alive with Christ, raising me with him, seating me with him at your right hand, establishing me in his authority, and anointing me with your love and your Spirit and your favor. I receive it all with thanks and give it total claim to my life—my spirit, soul, and body, my heart, mind, and will.

Dear God,

Speak gently in my silence.
When the loud outer noises of my surroundings and
the loud inner noises of my fears
Keep pulling me away from you,
Help me to trust that you are still there
even when I am unable to hear you.
Give me ears to listen to your small, soft voice saying:
"Come to me, you who are overburdened,
and I will give you rest....
For I am gentle and humble of heart."
Let that loving voice be my guide.

Amen[17]

—**Henri Nouwen**

PART TWO

◆

LOVING GOD

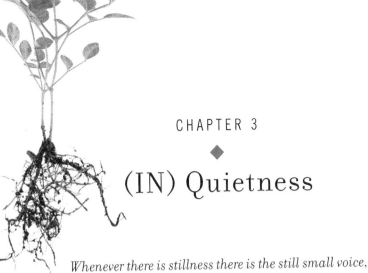

CHAPTER 3

◆

(IN) Quietness

Whenever there is stillness there is the still small voice,
God's speaking from the whirlwind, nature's old song, and dance...
—ANNIE DILLARD[1]

WE WERE RECREATING A TRIP through southern Germany and Austria, taken by my mom, dad, grandparents, aunt, and uncle when my parents were newlyweds. I'd heard about this trip, taken by car along the Romantic Road, at nearly every family gathering growing up. If we were all together long enough and the adults were on a second or third cocktail, the stories from this trip would bubble up with laughter and warmth. I'd dreamed of recreating this trip with my parents to hear their stories firsthand, to see where they'd lived as newlyweds while my dad was in the army. To share the sights, smells, sounds, and tastes of their adventure. My disconnected soul longed to connect with something of the past, to make my family story part of my story.

The scenic trip was magical and beautiful, a stepping back in time. We'd been in so many shops, churches, restaurants. We'd seen beautiful works of art, paintings, and wood carvings. Yet, this one stopped me, held me. I stood before a wood carving of the Last Supper that filled the altar space at the front of the little church in this picturesque medieval village. At the center of the image were John and Jesus, John's head resting against Jesus' chest. The intimacy of the friendship captured by the carver called to my soul. I drew breath in and held it, feeling an ache, a longing. I wanted that same space, my cheek pressing against his chest, hearing his heartbeat, to be held by the very heartbeat of God.

Jesus holds this same position with the Father. By John's account, "No one has ever seen God, but the one and only Son, who is himself God and is in closest relationship with the Father, has made him known."[2] The word in Greek translated here "closest relationship" is the word for "bosom," the chest of God. Jesus is in the very chest of God, one with the heartbeat of the Father.

John referred to himself in his gospel as "the one Jesus loved." Clearly, he felt he was Jesus' favorite. And so are we all. We all can hold this listening space with Jesus. Because we all are the one he loves. We are all held in the Father's heart.

Sometimes when I pray now, I feel this closeness. I see myself leaning in against Jesus' chest, my head tucked in under his chin. And I can sense his chest against my cheek, his arms around me. It is a place of deep rest. Peace. Quiet. Right up against the heartbeat of God. I've sought this place in prayer, and it has become with time a place I can return to. I think God has a place, even places, like this for all of us. Deeply personal places where we can meet and rest and listen.

John, known as the beloved disciple, began his first letter with these words: "That which was from the beginning, which we have heard, which we have seen with our eyes, which we have looked at and our hands have touched—this we proclaim concerning the Word of life."[3] He had heard Jesus, seen him, touched him, even rested against him. And this Jesus John calls the Word of life, God speaking to us in the form and voice of a man. John's experience was tangible, real, alive. Ours can be, too. Because God, the Word of life, is still speaking. And when I draw close and quiet to listen, I can feel my cheek against his chest and hear the beat of the sacred presence.

Because this presence is held within me as I am held within him. He is so close I can hear him.

A DAY IN THE LIFE

Jesus lived deeply connected with his Father, withdrawing often to remote places to pray. This rhythm of withdrawing from the crowds, even from the friends he traveled with, was essential to him. People were constantly pressing in, hoping for healing, for food, or for teaching that was different from anything they'd ever heard. Jesus could have spent all his days running frantically from city to city to meet an unending sea of need. But these needs did not drive his life. His connection with God rooted his life in a rhythm of rest. His Father's voice restored, blessed, affirmed. "This is my Son, whom I love; with him I am well pleased."[4] His Father's voice formed the inner reality of Jesus' life.

This listening connection fostered inward certainty. Jesus knew clearly who he was and what he was here to do. He knew because he was listening. "Very truly I tell you, the Son can do nothing by himself; he can do only what he sees his Father doing, because whatever the Father does the Son also does. For the Father loves the Son and shows him all he does."[5] As a human like us, filled with Spirit like us, Jesus lived rooted in prayer, listening moment by moment for what came next.

Our days are demanding, too. All the noise and busyness and fullness of our day's work disconnect us from the source of our life—the real, deep, solid life we long for. Sometimes all the noise drowns out the longing and we can't hear it anymore. We can't hear our hearts. We can't hear God. Returning to the place of hearing, listening to what is deepest and truest, we begin to connect again, to know ourselves. To know God. To know what to do next.

In the quiet place of presence, we silence our lives to listen for the living Word. We make sacred space in our day to connect, because we long to hear the words of wisdom and grace that sustain, direct, heal. In this place, condemnation and accusation are drowned in living water. In this place we are grounded again in love. It can happen in a moment. Just stop, breathe, listen.

I'd been following Jesus for years before I realized that prayer was about more than talking. With more years, I realized that prayer begins (and ends) with listening. Mother Teresa knew this to be true. She said, "God speaks in the silence of the heart. Listening is the beginning of prayer."[6] This kind of prayer is a conversation between friends—close friends who can hold silence together. Cheek-to-chest kind of friends who abide together, exchanging honest words with intimate knowing of the other. This listening connection is essential as we seek to live a life rooted and grounded in love.

Most of what I had heard about prayer in church centered on asking and keeping detailed lists of requests and answers. It was about me talking to God. A lot. To someone who comes at relationship through doing, and likes to be able to do things well, this sounds right and good and doable. I will log my prayer requests by category—family, friends, my community, my church, the world (there's a lot of asking to do)—and dutifully offer these requests to the Lord, sometimes with my very helpful thoughts about the best way for him to answer these prayers, just in case he needs suggestions. And I'll be encouraged and give thanks when I see prayers answered. It's neat and tidy and very doable. But it does not nourish my soul.

I was also aware that, from time to time, I'd feel nudges to do something, talk to someone, read a certain psalm or scripture. Sometimes I would know something about someone I didn't really have any way of knowing, or I'd have a dream that seemed to have meaning for my life. But I was completely unaware that these nudges and intuitions and dreams often came from God. God was speaking, trying to communicate with me, and I had no idea I was supposed to be listening.

Listening makes room for dialogue in relationship. We share our heart with God. He shares his heart with us. As we grow in know-ing and being known, friendship and trust deepen. We come to know God and to know ourselves better in the listening. And his prayers become our prayers as his heart becomes our heart.

ALL EAR

Jesus invited Peter, James, and John the beloved to join him, apart from the others, for a glimpse of his true self, the self that tran-scended time and space and the limitations of his temporary fleshly tent. They saw Jesus transfigured in dazzling white speaking with Moses and Elijah. The three disciples were stunned and dazed. I'm sure I would have been, too. And in this moment of revealed glory, they heard the Father speak: "This is my beloved son. Listen to him."[7]

Listen to him. It's an invitation to join our hearts with his. And in this invitation is a promise confirmed by Jesus.

> I have much more to say to you, more than you can now
> bear. But when he, the Spirit of truth, comes, he will guide
> you into all truth. He will not speak on his own; he will
> speak only what he hears, and he will tell you what is yet to
> come. He will bring glory to me by taking from what is mine
> and making it known to you. All that belongs to the Father
> is mine. That is why I said the Spirit will take from what is
> mine and make it known to you.[8]

All that belongs to the Father belongs to Jesus. The Spirit of God takes from all that belongs to Jesus and makes it known to us. The Spirit speaks what he hears to lead us into all truth. All truth. All. This is big, people. There's more available to us than we know. And it's available in the place of listening.

This promise is hard for us to believe for many reasons. We doubt ourselves and our ability to hear. We might get it wrong, after all. It would be easier if we heard an audible voice. Most of us never will. Instead, we hear, sense, are aware within of thoughts that don't seem like our thoughts. And we hear these thoughts, this inner voice, right along with the voices of culture, media, friends, family, the inner lies we believe, and a spiritual enemy who seeks to destroy us. It's a lot to sort out. And yet, Jesus says we will know his voice. We can know. Yes, we'll miss it sometimes. But we can know.

> The gatekeeper opens the gate for him, and the sheep listen to his voice. He calls his own sheep by name and leads them out. When he has brought out all his own, he goes on ahead of them, and his sheep follow him because they know his voice. But they will never follow a stranger; in fact, they will run away from him because they do not recognize a stranger's voice. . . . My sheep listen to my voice; I know them, and they follow me.[9]

I prayed with a young man several years ago who insisted he could not hear God speak to him. As my friend and I listened to his story, we could understand why. As a young boy, he'd been beaten and verbally abused by his father and brother. His earthly father's voice was hard, cruel, demeaning. How could he trust that his Heavenly Father's voice would be different? We made some progress in prayer in our first two sessions, but again and again, he said he could hear nothing for himself.

In our third session, as I was about to give up, I asked him to report to us the first thing that came to mind when we asked God what he wanted this young man to know about what he had experienced. The first thing—no editing or discounting. Even if the first thing that came to mind was "pink elephant," I asked him to share it. We would figure out together if it was God or not. He agreed. We asked the Lord to help him connect. I held my breath and asked the question. "God, what do you want him to know about what happened to him? How do you feel about that?" I waited a moment in silence; then asked him what came to mind.

"All I hear is scripture."

He began to tell us the scriptures that came to mind, beautiful words of God's love and redemption. And he was discounting them because he'd memorized these scriptures and more. He'd memorized hundreds of verses. For years he had been hiding these words in his heart. And now God was speaking to him through these very words, living words. It was beautiful. And he'd almost missed it.

"That's God," we said to him. "These are his words to you today." He looked doubtful for a moment; then a smile spread across his face. "Let's keep listening and see what else God wants to show you."

Now he was (IN), and this simple validation that God really was speaking to him opened the door to more. Within minutes, he said he saw a wall dividing him from Jesus. Jesus began to show him what the wall was made of, the hurt and pain of his past, and the healing journey for this young man opened up as the wall began to come down.

"Faith comes from hearing, and hearing through the word of Christ."[10] Our faith, our trust in God, comes as we hear. The Greek word for "word" in this verse from the book of Romans means that which is or has been uttered by the living voice of Jesus. Our ability to believe and live in truth about God and about us depends on hearing. Listening births faith, the soil of trust from which new life grows.

Theologian, professor, and prolific writer Henri Nouwen invites us to live "all ear" like Jesus:

> From all that I said about our worried, overfilled lives, it is clear that we are usually surrounded by so much outer noise that it is hard to truly hear our God when he is speaking to us. We have often become deaf, unable to know when God calls us and unable to understand in which direction he calls us.

Thus our lives have become absurd. In the word *absurd* we find the Latin word *surdus*, which means "deaf." A spiritual life requires discipline because we need to learn to listen to God, who constantly speaks but whom we seldom hear.

When, however, we learn to listen, our lives become obedient lives. The word *obedient* comes from the Latin word *audire*, which means "listening." A spiritual discipline is necessary in order to move slowly from an absurd to an obedient life, from a life filled with noisy worries to a life in which there is some free inner space where we can listen to our God and follow his guidance.

Jesus' life was a life of obedience. He was always listening to the Father, always attentive to his voice, always alert for his directions. Jesus was "all ear." That is true prayer: being all ear for God. The core of all prayer is indeed listening, obediently standing in the presence of God.[11]

HEARING GOD

Samuel, a young Hebrew boy, lived in a time when the word of the Lord was rarely heard. As assistant to the priest Eli in the temple, Samuel slept by the ark of God. It would be hard to get closer to the place where God was present to his people, since this was God's address at the time. Late one night, two times Samuel heard a voice call to him, two times he ran to Eli, and two times Eli sent him back to bed. The third time Samuel came running, Eli realized what was happening. The Lord was calling to Samuel. Eli sent Samuel back to lie down and listen. "[If God] calls you, say, 'Speak, LORD, for your servant is listening.' So Samuel went and lay down in his place. The LORD came and stood there, calling as at the other times, 'Samuel! Samuel!' Then Samuel said, 'Speak, for your servant is listening.'"[12] Samuel wasn't familiar with the Lord's voice; it sounded to him like Eli. At first, we may not be familiar with it either. We may mistake it for our own internal voice, or we may miss it altogether. But when we recognize the source and tune in, like Samuel, we have an encounter with the God who speaks.

For centuries, people have heard the word of the Lord through the Scriptures. These books, letters, poems, and proverbs, breathed by God and inspired by Spirit, speak to our hearts and help us understand the mind and will of God. These same Scriptures are filled with stories of people hearing God speak in an audible voice, in a gentle whisper, in visions and dreams, through the wonder of creation, through other people and prophets, through their own thoughts and imaginations, and even through Balaam's ass.[13]

God is eager to speak with you in one or more of these ways right now. (Probably not through a donkey.) But maybe you, like the young man we prayed with, don't feel like you can hear. What's in the way? Beliefs, expectations, fears, disappointments, even spiritual dynamics can block or hinder our connection with God.

- A belief: "God doesn't speak like that today."
- Expectations and disappointment: "I've tried. I just don't hear from God."
- Comparisons: "I don't hear from God like they do."
- Fear: "I might get it wrong."
- Guilt or shame: "I'm not worthy enough."

Does one or more of these statements ring true for you? If so, you have an opportunity to dialogue with God about how you're feeling and what you're believing. Read the words of Jesus again. He says his Spirit comes to speak. He promises we'll know his voice. The very thing blocking you is an invitation to step through into a new, more open space with him—a space not limited to words on a page.

Pastor and author A. W. Tozer said we make a mistake when we refer only to the Bible as the Word of God. "True, the inspired Bible is the Word of God speaking to our hearts and to our souls. But in referring to the Word of God, we do not mean just the book—printed pages sewed together with nylon thread. Rather, we mean the eternal expression of the mind of God. We mean the world-filling breath of God!"[14]

THE SOUND OF HIS VOICE

Eve and Adam knew the sound of God in the garden. How do we know what God sounds like? How do we discern if we're really hearing the voice of God, or if our fear or anxiety or the pizza we ate last night is speaking to us? A few questions can help:

- What's the tone? Is it loving? Encouraging? Or does it carry the sting of accusation?
- What's the content? Does it sound like something Jesus would say?
- Do trusted friends confirm what you're hearing?

God's voice sounds like Jesus. And most of what Jesus said and did was completely unexpected. He repeatedly confused his listeners with his parables. He challenged and offended religious leaders. He shared his life with outcasts. He chose the unchosen. Touched the untouchables. His words brought comfort to some and made others very uncomfortable. All in the name of love.

On a journey from Judea to Galilee, Jesus stopped at a well in Samaria to rest in the heat of the day.[15] His friends had gone off to get food, and as Jesus waited there, a woman approached the well to get water. This woman didn't come with the other women in the cool of the day. She came separately, at midday, because she was an outcast in her community. Normally, a Jewish rabbi would not address a Samaritan or a woman or a "sinner." Jesus shocks the woman (and his friends) by asking her for a drink. He confuses her by offering her living water. Then he reveals he knows she is now living with a man who is not her husband—and in fact, she's had five husbands. Ultimately, he shares himself with her in a way he chooses not to with most others. He tells her he is the Messiah.

Jesus surprises her. He confuses her mind. Challenges her

beliefs. Reveals her heart. All to invite her to life, to drink living water. All to reveal himself as the one she has been waiting for. The woman goes home to tell the story of her encounter with Jesus, and many put their faith in him. Through this unorthodox exchange, this woman who was an outcast is restored to community.

God does the same with us. As we listen, he will surprise, confuse, challenge, and reveal our heart and motives. And he does it all to invite, to heal, to reveal, to restore the very thing we need for life. His words are not always comfortable or expected or orthodox, but they bring comfort because they come with love to offer living water.

God is still speaking today by his Spirit, sustaining us, holding us, keeping us by his word just as the vine holds the branch. As I quiet my life to listen, God's words, living and active, pierce my heart in love to remove the things that hinder, to reveal what's hidden to heal. His living word lands with love to take root in my soul. Hearing God's word for ourselves, spoken into the circumstances of our lives, into the good and bad—this is the game-changer. In this place of deep connection, we experience truth and grace, and the channels of living water, of life and healing, are opened. We must hear to heal, to live, to thrive.

DEEPER (IN)

How do we cultivate a listening life? We tune in and learn to recognize God speaking to us with practice. As you ask God to give you ears to hear and eyes to see, and as you open more space in your life for silence and solitude, your experience of hearing God will increase.

In the coming week, try these two practices. Consider how each is helpful, and how you might include one or both in a rhythm of prayer.

Lectio Divina—Ephesians 3:16–21

Lectio Divina is sacred reading, a way of listening to the written word with the heart. Richard Foster describes it as "the kind of reading in which the mind descends into the heart and both are drawn into the love and goodness of God."[16]

To begin, select a passage. For this first exercise, I suggest Ephesians 3:16–21. Find the verses in a Bible or online (or in Chapter 1). Read the passage aloud four times, slowly and deliberately. Between each reading, allow a time of silence to let the words permeate your heart.

> **Read**: On the first reading, simply listen to the words read aloud.
>
> **Reflect**: On the second reading, ask: What in the passage touches my life today?
>
> **Respond**: After the third reading, ask yourself: What is God inviting me to today?
>
> **Rest**: During the fourth and final reading, ask nothing; simply rest in the presence of the Lord.

Listening Prayer with Journaling

Writing your conversations with God can help you listen. Pull out a notebook, journal, or sheet of paper. You might begin simply by writing about how you're feeling, your concerns, things you're thankful for. Whatever comes to mind. This is your conversation with God, so be honest and real. What question comes to mind as you write? Write your question. Then stop, breathe, and listen. What do you sense from God? What thoughts come to mind? Write what you're sensing. Try not to worry too much just yet if it's all God or not. You can figure that out later. For now, just write. Keep the conversation going. What's your response to him? What's his response to you? Where do you need wisdom? Where do you need encouragement? You are sitting with a friend. Enjoy the honest conversation. Be ready for surprises. Be ready for love.

The next day, come back to what you wrote. Read it again prayerfully. Highlight or underline what stands out to you. Do some parts sound more like God? Do some parts sound more like you? What feels most important or rises to the top? Hold these thoughts before Jesus and ask if there's more he wants to say.

◆

(IN) Trust

...to be trusted is a greater compliment
than to be loved.
—GEORGE MACDONALD[1]

MY FATHER WAS SOBBING.

I'd rarely seen my father cry. I remember anger. Laughter. Acts of kindness. Silence. Absence. But never tears.

I'd come downstairs to find him completely undone, emotions spilling everywhere. I was living at home after graduating from college. Not because I wanted to—I had searched for a job in Nashville but come up empty. So here I was, living in the condo I would draw a few years later on the counselor's whiteboard. Unable like so many others to find my real job, I was working retail at Macy's and applying for anything even remotely related to the field of publishing. And there is not a lot of publishing to be found in Cincinnati. So it was taking a while.

My father looked distraught. "I need to talk to you. I'm so sorry. Please forgive me." I had no idea what he was talking about. Forgive him for what? He had never in my life said he was sorry or wrong or apologized for anything.

"Every day when you were little you would run to the door to greet me and ask to play when I came home from work. One day when you ran to the door, I said, 'Susan, I'm not your friend. I'm your father.' I sent you away. That was the last time you ever ran to the door. I'm so sorry. Please forgive me."

I was stunned. I had no conscious memory of this happening. But in an instant, so many things in my life made sense. Missing pieces of a puzzle fell into place filling in the landscape of my childhood. The isolation. The sense of never being chosen. The little girl rejected by her father. "I'm not your friend." Friend and father would be forever separated in my little girl heart.

I told my father that I had no memory of what he was telling me, which seemed to be a relief to him. I told him I forgave him. He cried and hugged me and thanked me. Told me he wanted to make amends. And for a day or two, I believed him.

Little changed in our relationship. As the child of two alcoholic parents, raised by an aunt, and moved from place to place, a street kid who learned how to survive on his own, he just didn't know how. How could he know? He was angry and disconnected for good reasons. For all of us, there are reasons we do the things we do. It would take several years and more healing for me to fully forgive and receive my dad's tears and repentance as deep and real and born from love. For now, the little girl was still angry and hurt and afraid to trust.

Perhaps my presence back at home for a few months was prompting some soul-searching within my dad. He was reaching across the distance in our relationship to try to bridge the gap. Not long after this, we were having lunch together. He was a car salesman—one job in a long string of many—and was helping me buy a new car. We were talking about cars one minute. The next, he was apologizing. He told me he was sorry he'd put so much pressure on me as a child to excel. He said he'd always known from the first time he held me that I would do something significant in life. He pushed me because he knew I could do great things. Now in hindsight, he realized he'd pushed too hard.

You could have knocked me right out of that booth at Steak 'n Shake with your pinky. You mean my internalized perfectionism and people-pleasing actually came from somewhere? (It pretty much always comes from somewhere.) I had no idea. I don't remember my dad being demanding about grades or activities. Maybe I'd placed all those memories neatly in my subconscious, right alongside the scene at the front door. I don't know. But it was the first time I heard my father say I was special and that he believed I would do great things. That knowledge was a gift. The father's blessing was healing balm.

With my father's confessions, I was now aware of what my soul had known all these years. My little girl heart and mind had assigned meaning to my father's actions that day, to that act and to many other acts—some intentional, many not. With the meaning came messages that shaped my view of myself and of my father. When I was turned away at the door that day, father and friend were separated. And with the breaking of innocent child trust, my image of myself and of God was darkened.

OUR IMAGE OF GOD

Experiences with fathers and authority figures color our image of God, for better and for worse. As a young girl, my image of father had been colored with a few different crayons. Distant. Angry. Demanding. Absent. But also, at times, protecting and fun and kind. I had only a few, mostly darker crayons to color father in my emotional crayon box. And these were the colors I brought into my relationship with God. Except I didn't know it. My image of God and how he loved me was colored with crayons that didn't make a very pretty picture. This was not a picture I could trust.

Over the years of my own healing journey and of participating in the healing journeys of so many others, I've seen brokenness in many forms. Broken hearts, broken bodies, broken minds, broken emotions. The fruit of our brokenness comes in many flavors and colors. But the roots are so very much the same. At the center of our beings, at the core, we believe two lies to varying degrees, simultaneously. We don't believe God is completely good. And we don't believe we are completely loved. These are the lies that kill our hearts, our minds, our bodies.

Our experiences in this life teach us that love is conditional and God may be, well, sketchy. Kind and healing one moment. But then disaster strikes, and we are not so sure. And we live from this experience, from the disappointments and woundings of life. We live from the pain of being rejected by father at the door. We live rooted, abiding in the false rather than the true, and our hearts become sick as we draw death into our very souls.

If you're a church person, you've probably heard, read, and even sung that God is good. But deep within, maybe you're not really sure. Read or watch the news. It's pretty bleak out there. Our hope is deferred. A lot. And our hearts are sick. Personal disappointments. Sickness. Wars. Refugees. Poverty. Riots. Deep prejudice and hate. Abuse. Terrorism. Politics (don't get me started). It gets pretty ugly. Add to that a long list of prayers that seem as yet unanswered. All point to a God who is angry or distant or inconstant in love.

We seek healing of our body and soul because we want relief from our pain, the pain of living in a broken world. We hear stories of Jesus healing, restoring. And yet part of us wonders, will God heal, will he restore this time? Does he really want to? We wonder if God is really this good. And we wonder if we really deserve his goodness. Our view of God and of ourselves is skewed. And the skew, this distortion of truth, gets in the way.

How we see ourselves and how we see God—the seeing of both is intrinsically connected. A. W. Tozer said it this way: "What comes into our minds when we think about God is the most important thing about us."[2] When we see ourselves, believe ourselves to be alone, unloved, unchosen, unworthy, we find ourselves unable to trust the One who is love. Love seeks a place in the soil of our soul to take root and grow, but so much of our heart is already rooted in the false, the lie of unlove. As ground opens in our heart for love, as we are able to receive unconditional, unearned, unqualified love from God, we add colors to our emotional crayon boxes. Our image of God becomes brighter, stronger, kinder, as we begin to experience the unwavering, unrelenting love of a God who is always good, always worthy of our trust.

IN JESUS

Jesus said, if you've seen me, you've seen the Father.[3] It's easier to see God's beauty and goodness in Jesus. He's healing, feeding the hungry, loving the outcast, sacrificing his life in love. Jesus seems like someone we can trust. Author and ragamuffin Brennan Manning expresses it this way:

> We cannot deduce anything about Jesus from what we think we know about God; however, we must deduce everything about God from what we know about Jesus. This implies that all of our prevailing images and understandings of God must crumble in the earthquake of Jesus' self-disclosure. Trust means the willingness to become absolutely empty of all terrifying and comforting images of God that we have held, so that the gift of God in Jesus Christ may come to us on God's terms.[4]

Jesus was showing and telling about his father all the time. In a story of a father and two sons, he paints a picture for us.[5] One son asked for his share of the inheritance that would be due to him upon his father's death. It was a brash request, the ultimate rejection of his father and family. His father, still very much alive, granted the request, and the son took off to live a life of wine, women, and song. Until the money ran out. And the son realized, as he was eating scraps with pigs, that his father's servants had a better life than he had. He decided to return home, apologize to his father, and live as a servant. He had spent all the privileges that had been his as a son.

> But while he was still a long way off, his father saw him and was filled with compassion for him; he ran to his son, threw his arms around him and kissed him.
>
> The son said to him, "Father, I have sinned against heaven and against you. I am no longer worthy to be called your son."
>
> But the father said to his servants, "Quick! Bring the best robe and put it on him. Put a ring on his finger and sandals on his feet. Bring the fattened calf and kill it. Let's have a feast and celebrate. For this son of mine was dead and is alive again; he was lost and is found." So they began to celebrate.

The father rejoices over his son, returning him to his place in the family. The robe, ring, and sandals are all signs that his sonship is restored. And the party begins. Are you following? God is throwing a party because his son has come home.

All this really ticks off the older brother who has been working faithfully for his father the whole time. He is having none of this. The father begs him to join the party, and this son stubbornly refuses. "Look! All these years I've been slaving for you and never disobeyed your orders. Yet you never gave me even a young goat so I could celebrate with my friends. But when this son of yours who has squandered your property with prostitutes comes home, you kill the fattened calf for him!" The older brother is angry and indignant at the generosity and goodness of his father.

"'My son,' the father said, 'you are always with me, and every-thing I have is yours. But we had to celebrate and be glad, because this brother of yours was dead and is alive again; he was lost and is found.'"

"You are always with me, and everything I have is yours." For both sons, this was true. Nothing they had done—or not done—had changed this. But neither of them knew it. Neither of them really knew their father at all. The first son thought he'd lost his place in the family. The second son thought he had to earn his place in the family. Neither knew they were (IN) the father's love, always with him, all the time. The father's love, his goodness, kindness, generosity never changed.

The life of Jesus and the stories he tells invite us to trust the good-ness of the Father, to think differently about God. When Jesus calls people to repent, he uses the Greek word *metanoeo*, which means to think differently. To have a different thought about what's true. Jesus is inviting us to think, to see God, to relate to God differently. Not through our behavior. This relationship isn't based on what we do or don't do. This relationship is based solely on turning, trusting, choosing to step into what has been true the whole time. God is not transactional, waiting for us to do or not do the right thing so he'll turn to us. He is relational, the father always ready to throw a party. He is always with us, turned toward us, simply waiting for us to turn, to return to him, to choose trust.

TRUST AND THE TRUTH

"You are always with me, and everything I have is yours." This God who throws parties in our honor invites us to trust.

In order to trust, we need to know this is true. Maybe not fully know it, because I'm not sure yet when exactly that happens. But there must be a mustard-seed-sized belief (just the tiniest grain), growing in the middle of all the doubt and wondering, declaring within us that God really is this good. And even that belief, that faith, comes by gift, comes from God. The work of love and trust begins and ends with him.

This trust requires honesty. This trust looks straight into what is real today and prays. Not flowery prayers that defy reality, but raw, visceral prayers that cry out for encounter. And in this place of prayer—talking, crying, screaming, listening, thanking, releasing—God's goodness becomes rooted in us.

David, king of Israel, knew this to be true. The psalms he wrote are filled with strong, honest emotion. David held nothing back.

> My God, my God, why have you forsaken me?
> Why are you so far from saving me,
> so far from my cries of anguish?
> My God, I cry out by day, but you do not answer,
> by night, but I find no rest.
> Yet you are enthroned as the Holy One;
> you are the one Israel praises.
> In you our ancestors put their trust;
> they trusted and you delivered them.
> To you they cried out and were saved;
> in you they trusted and were not put to shame.
> But I am a worm and not a man,
> scorned by everyone, despised by the people.
> All who see me mock me;
> they hurl insults, shaking their heads.
> "He trusts in the LORD," they say,
> "let the LORD rescue him.
> Let him deliver him,
> since he delights in him."
> Yet you brought me out of the womb;
> you made me trust in you, even at my mother's breast.
> From birth I was cast on you;
> from my mother's womb you have been my God.
> Do not be far from me,

for trouble is near
and there is no one to help.[6]

This is the prayer of a man who knows God is good, faithful, near. Yet the conflict is real. He expresses his fear, anger, anguish honestly. "You do not answer." He asks real questions. "Why have you forsaken me?" He makes real requests. "Do not be far from me . . . there is no one to help." He expresses his pain fully and powerfully.

I am poured out like water,
and all my bones are out of joint.
My heart has turned to wax;
it has melted within me.[7]

David does not edit or deny his agony. He brings his heart fully and honestly before God. He invites God to meet him in the middle of trouble, doubt, fear. And in this meeting of hearts—David's heart and God's—David's trust is renewed.

I will declare your name to my people;
in the assembly I will praise you.
You who fear the LORD, praise him!
All you descendants of Jacob, honor him!
Revere him, all you descendants of Israel!
For he has not despised or scorned
the suffering of the afflicted one;
he has not hidden his face from him
but has listened to his cry for help.[8]

With this prayer, David moves from isolation and separation to connection. From feeling forsaken to knowing God is present. God has not hidden his face. God has seen. God has listened. This is the connecting, transforming power of real prayer, our honest conversation with God. This is trust.

"My God, my God, why have you forsaken me?" Jesus prays this part of David's prayer on the cross as he is tortured and dying. Jesus, who is inseparably connected with his Father, one with God, the very likeness of God, cries out in real anguish, with a very honest question. It's our question, too. God, where are you in this pain, in this mess? Why have you abandoned me? Do you hear me? Do you see? Where is my help?

Trust is not a religious declaration that denies reality. Religion and denial are rooted in shame and fear. Trust is rooted in the safety and constancy of God's love. Trust says with the apostle John, "We ourselves have known and put our trust in God's love toward ourselves."[9] Trust invites this love right into the middle of what is real. Right into the middle of the mess, the anguish, the pain, the cursing, the doubt. And this invitation, this trust, this prayer is the place of encounter. God, the one who is love, can only be present in this singular, very true, real, honest, messy moment.

"You are always with me. Everything I have is yours."

HEALING OUR IMAGE OF GOD

The French celebrate Easter with the phrase, *L'amour de Dieu est folie!*—God's love is God's folly. The love of God—the love expressed in the life, death, and Easter resurrection of Jesus—makes no rational sense. It is unconditional. Bigger, wider, higher, deeper than we can know. (Remember our prayer from Ephesians 3?) It creates, restores, forgives, lives, dies, and lives again, all and always for the other. It enters our humanity, embraces our nakedness, offends the religious, and defies our logic. God's love is the expression of surpassing goodness, unbounded mercy. We need to experience this love, this God, desperately.

We tend to think, act, pray as if God is like what we've seen and experienced with the fathers and mothers and authorities around us. But God is above and beyond anything we've known, the one who is infinite, boundless, extravagant love. The one who looks and loves and gives like Jesus. He is always greater, always other—and in the end, always mystery. But he can be known and longs to be known, and this knowing comes in experience.

To restore our image of God, we must re-see the painful experiences and images that have misshaped and mis-colored our view of him. After my dad shared the story of his rejection of me at the front door, I began to wonder how that had shaped my life, colored my view of God and of myself. My experience of father was very different from the father in Jesus' story. The father of the younger son met him with open arms, restored him, threw him a party. This father was unchanging in his love. This father could be trusted. "You are always with me. Everything I have is yours."

So one day I asked. Jesus, that day, there at the door, how do you respond to me? How do you receive me? I saw us there. Me, the little girl. Jesus, the father at the door. He smiled broadly, swept me up in his arms, and took me outside to play. Without hesitation and with all joy. And in that moment, father and friend were one again. I felt his joy, his love. I experienced his goodness in a way that made it true, truer than my mind could ever know. It was now true in my core, the very center of my being. This new picture, this experience, is bigger and stronger and truer than what I'd experienced with my dad. It stays with me. It's changed and is changing me. Because I know I can trust this Father's love.

> But blessed is the one who trusts in the LORD,
> whose confidence is in him.
> They will be like a tree planted by the water
> that sends out its roots by the stream.
> It does not fear when heat comes;
> its leaves are always green.
> It has no worries in a year of drought
> and never fails to bear fruit.[10]

DEEPER (IN)

Imaginative Prayer

Ignatian prayer emphasizes the power of the restored imagination to deepen our relationship with God. One form of prayer in the Spiritual Exercises of St. Ignatius focuses on engaging our imagination in prayerful reflection on scenes from the Gospels. In this exercise, we are invited to participate in the story, to engage our senses and emotions, and to experience the sights, smells, sounds of the scene. We're invited to watch how Jesus is present to us and to others in the story.

In this exercise, you'll use the Ignatian practice of imaginative prayer with the story of the father and the two sons in Luke 15:11–32. Find the story in your Bible or online. Then dial down. Close your eyes. Take a few deep, slow breaths. Invite God to be present with you and to you in the story. Ask him to help you see and experience him.

Open your eyes and read the story, slowly, a few verses at a time. Read a few verses. Then close your eyes and picture it. Engage your senses. What do you see? Who do you see? How does it smell, feel, taste? Take your time. Where are you in the story? Where is the Father? Read a few more verses and stop to engage again. What emotions do you feel? How is the Father meeting you? Continue with a few verses at a time until you complete the story.

Reflect (maybe even write, color, draw, paint) on your experience. How does the way you've seen and encountered father in this prayer compare with your view of God? How does this experience of the father help you begin to reimage God and his love for you? How do you see him differently? How do you see yourself differently? If it feels helpful, return to this story and invite the Father to continue to help you re-see him and re-see yourself.

Writing a Psalm

Many of the psalms written by King David follow the pattern of Psalm 22. They begin with lament. They are honest and raw, full of questions and complaints. Then they take a turn to trust, remembering the goodness and faithfulness of God. Write your own psalm. Be real. Hold nothing back. Leave nothing unsaid. Invite God into the middle of it. All of it. And as you write, wait for trust to rise. You might just be surprised by the turn your psalm takes.

◆

CHAPTER 5

(IN) Rest

Almost everything will work again if you unplug it
for a few minutes, including you.
—ANNE LAMOTT[1]

"CAN YOU FEEL THAT?"

I had never been very vigilant about breast self-exams. Partly, I was sure I wouldn't find anything. Partly, I was afraid I would. Mostly, I don't think I had confidence in my ability to find whatever it was I was supposed to be looking for. But I had always been vigilant about my annual trips to my OB-GYN. And, since the age of thirty-nine when my doctor sent me for my baseline mammogram, I had been faithful. A few moments of uncomfortable squishing were far outweighed by the assurance that I was healthy. And any sense of modesty I might have had in my life had been annihilated by the process of childbirth.

I was in, by all accounts, excellent health. Sure, a few (OK, maybe more like fifteen) extra pounds still remained on my frame after the birth of my daughter, Virginia. But I exercised faithfully and ate a pretty healthy diet. I had no major health problems. I had no family history of breast cancer. I had, I thought, nothing to worry about.

"Can you feel that?"

Dr. Grim (such an unfortunate name for a doctor, right?) was pressing in on the outside of my right breast. I placed my hand in the same spot and pressed. I felt nothing—at first. Then a tiny hard mass—like a small pea. Yes, I felt it.

I searched his eyes for assurance. "It feels like a cyst," he said. "Probably nothing to worry about. We'll send you in for a mammogram, just to be sure." The words brought comfort. I was confident still that I had nothing to worry about. Cysts were common enough.

A few days later I was in position to be smooshed, squeezed, and scanned. They took one set of pictures. Then another. "Don't worry," the nurse said. "The doctor almost always wants to see a second set—just to be sure."

The nurse came back a third time and said the doctor now wanted an ultrasound. For the first time, I felt afraid. I sat in my gown in the small dressing room waiting for the ultrasound technician. And I prayed. "God. Please. Help." Nothing profound in the prayer, but it came from a gasp deep in my gut, as most real prayer does. I pulled my heart back from fear and pushed my thoughts toward God.

"You won't get an answer today. And it will be all right." The words formed clearly in my mind. I knew these were not my words. And I knew that my definition of "all right" and God's were often very different. But with the words came peace. Lord, I trust you. I trust you. I trust you.

The doctor looked at the screen and invited me to look, too. "See it?" Yes, I saw it. The spot was dark and too real to be denied. She was firm and direct. "It's not a cyst."

I was drowning in a sea of questions. "So what are my options?" I asked.

"We can schedule a biopsy for you. Or we can do a biopsy now." Her smile was kind, full of understanding. Biopsy. The word is a one-way ticket on the fear train. I was trying to make sense of it all.

"So I have a tumor. And now we just have to find out if it's benign or cancerous. Is that it?" Yes, that was it. For the first time, my mind entertained the word "cancer." "Do the biopsy now," I said. Waiting another day for another test would be simply more days of worry for me. If we

need to take action, then take action now. And so she began the proce-
dure for the biopsy. I watched it all on the screen. She was kind, care-
ful, thorough. And it was over.

"We will know tomorrow morning by 10:00," she said. "If you
haven't heard from me by then, call me directly." The doctor left. The
technician gave me a hug. I was done.

"You won't get an answer today. And it will be all right." The
whisper came soft and clear.

I dressed and called my husband. The tears came as I heard his
voice. I stood in the hall, trying not to sob as the waves of emotion hit
me. He was concerned, but calm. Dave is the glass-half-full part of
our marriage. Ever optimistic, he was confident of the best possible
outcome. As we talked, my emotions settled. I clung to the promise.
No matter what, "it will be all right."

The following morning as I prayed, God whispered into my heart
again. The words came strong and clear. "You have cancer. And it will
be all right." I was prepared for the worst, but still hoping, always hoping for the best. At 10:01, I picked up the phone in my office at church
and called the doctor. She came on the line quickly. "You have cancer."
God had prepared me. But I was totally unprepared. The words sounded
so odd, so wrong. It was almost as if my brain was trying to interpret a
foreign language. My entire reality shifted in a moment. The whisper
came again. "I will heal you, but you will have to go all the way." I knew
instantly what this meant. It meant no instantaneous miracle. Sometimes God and I have a very different idea of what "all right" looks like.

I was now compelled to go on a journey I did not choose or want.
Surgery. Chemo. Radiation. Hair loss. Sickness. Fatigue. I wanted none
of this. But if I was going to do cancer, I was going to do it well. Because
I'm an achiever, right? And the achiever in me determined to get an A
in cancer. I would learn from it. I would meet God in it. Make the most
of my recovery time. Memorize Scripture. Pray lots. Send out prayer
updates so people would be praying for me. I wouldn't be just a survivor.

I would thrive through this. (It's OK if you're laughing now. It's pretty ridiculous.)

My value was deeply rooted in all the doing, achieving, performing. Cancer stripped that away. It shoved me rudely from self-sufficiency to dependence, and it made me profoundly and painfully aware of my limitations. For days after each treatment I was unable to cook, clean, take care of my daughter, work, pray. Some days I was unable to read. And "chemo brain" made it impossible for me to think clearly, remember basics, or memorize anything. Unable to do all the things that typically gave my life meaning and value, I was left with just weak, needy me. And that did not feel like nearly enough.

I learned to ask for and receive help because I had to. For someone who measures her sense of worth by doing, achieving, succeeding, this was no easy task. The only thing I was succeeding at some days was making it from the bed to the couch for HGTV.

My identity was rooted in the doing. The lie of not enough drove me to do just a little more, to work just a little harder, all the time. In the darkness of cancer, I encountered the gift of my own undoing. Forced to rest, I found a place of stillness that opened the door to my soul. The noise of all the doing in my life was silenced, and I was left with, well, just me. Sick, tired, bald, unproductive me. And it turned out, just me was enough, without all the busyness of accomplishing and achieving and proving. It turned out I didn't have to prove anything. Because love isn't measured out a handful at a time, based on my doing. It is poured out lavishly without condition based solely on my connection to the one who is love. In weakness and rest, I found myself, and a healing deeper and fuller than any I'd known.

FINDING REST

We are so unaccustomed to the stillness of rest. It is so unproductive, after all. In truth, it makes most of us terribly uncomfortable. We fill our eyes and ears with a steady stream of media because we are afraid of the quiet. Twenty-four-hour news cycles, Twitter feeds, Facebook, Instagram, Snapchat, smartphones. We live noisy, busy lives—disconnected, overly full lives—because we fear the quiet. If we are still, we won't be seen, heard, pursued, valued. If we are still, we fear what might fill the empty space—the anxiety and self-doubt lurking just beneath the surface, ready to pounce. The voices telling us we're not enough. But the stillness isn't empty at all. It is, instead, the place of encounter, the place of presence. In stillness and in rest, we hear the voice that calms our fears and fills our emptiness. And in this place, we find ourselves.

When a successful Christian leader asked theologian Dallas Willard what one thing he'd recommend to bring new energy to his spiritual life, Willard replied, "You must ruthlessly eliminate hurry from your life, for hurry is the great enemy of spiritual life in our world today."[2] When the leader asked what else he'd recommend, Willard replied that there was nothing else. Ruthlessly eliminate hurry. The busyness. All the excessive doing. That was it. And that is all.

God invites us to live centered not in our doing, but in our being.

> In repentance and rest is your salvation,
> in quietness and trust is your strength,
> but you would have none of it.[3]

As we turn again to God, coming into rest and quietness and trust, connection is restored. We are restored. This invitation is such good news. And yet often we, like the people of Isaiah's time, will have none of it. We choose the noisy, busy, self-sufficient way.

"The biblical revelation," says Father Richard Rohr, "is about awakening, not accomplishing. You cannot get there, you can only be there, but the foundational Being-in-God, for some reason, is too hard to believe, and too good to be true for most people. Only the humble will usually believe it and receive it, because it affirms more about God than it does about us. Proud people are not attracted to such explanations."[4]

IN THE QUIET

The connection we long for, the sense of rootedness we seek, requires rest. But the space this opens for us is daunting; we feel the itch to fill it. We hear the noise of our soul, or what Henri Nouwen calls an inner chaos.

> To bring solitude into our lives is one of the most necessary but also most difficult disciplines. Even though we may have a deep desire for real solitude, we also experience a certain apprehension as we approach that solitary place and time. As soon as we are alone, without people to talk with, books to read, TV to watch, or phone calls to make, an inner chaos opens up in us.
>
> This chaos can be so disturbing and so confusing that we can hardly wait to get busy again. Entering a private room and shutting the door, therefore, does not mean we immediately shut out all our inner doubts, anxieties, fears, bad memories, unresolved conflicts, angry feelings, and impulsive desires. On the contrary, when we have removed our outer distractions, we often find that our inner distractions manifest themselves to us in full force.[5]

As we brave the chaos that rises in the stillness, we find ourselves and the love that carries us. In cancer, so much of the noisy false was stripped away. The things I held up to the world, to myself, even to God, to prove my worth. When all the overachieving and perfecting and striving fall away, in the dark, naked quiet, I find healing. Because I find that my worth isn't attached to the doing at all. It is all gift. Author Shauna Niequist writes:

> The only way through the emptiness is stillness: staring at the deep wound unflinchingly. You can't outrun anything.

I've tried. All you can do is show up in the stillness….When you begin to carry God's love and true peace deep within your actual soul like a treasure chest, you realize that you don't have to fling yourself around the planet searching for those things outside yourself. You only have to go back into the stillness to locate it. That treasure you've been searching for—for so long—was there all the time.[6]

The psalmist invites us to "Be still, and know."[7] Be still, and know God. Only in the stillness do we know, not with our heads but with our hearts, at the core of our very beings. Here we know God's character. The one who is love by nature and being, reveals his love. And we begin to experience it, to live in it, to live from it. Because it is here, with and within us, all the time.

Jesus invites us as well. "Come to me and I will give you rest." Eugene Petersen renders this invitation for us beautifully in *The Message*:

> Are you tired? Worn out? Burned out on religion? Come to me. Get away with me and you'll recover your life. I'll show you how to take a real rest. Walk with me and work with me—watch how I do it. Learn the unforced rhythms of grace. I won't lay anything heavy or ill-fitting on you. Keep company with me and you'll learn to live freely and lightly.[8]

As we learn this rhythm of rest with Jesus, we find what we long for. Just come. The rest you seek, the rest your soul craves, is here with him. Sit. Be. Rest. Receive the gift.

SOLITUDE AND SILENCE

I went on my first silent retreat about ten years ago. The thought of twenty-four hours of silence was daunting. I felt some trepidation. But my soul was weary and I was seeking rest. The leader, spiritual director Sibyl Towner, was preparing us for the experience. "The first thing you'll notice when you get quiet is how tired you are. And you will probably need to take a nap. This is holy rest." Seriously? I so love that! A nap can be holy. She gave us permission to rest, to sleep. Because we needed it—both the permission and the rest. Essential to connecting, to being present in the silence, was rest.

As we were released for the next twenty-four hours into silence, I felt it. Within the first ten minutes I felt how enormously tired my body was. I felt the distraction of my mind and the weariness of my soul. I was exhausted from the pushing, the doing, the mere act of living in a noisy, busy world. I slept. I sat in sun. I breathed in fresh air. I read. I listened. I prayed. I walked the prayer labyrinth. I ate. I slept again. Slowly, suddenly, a space opened in me that was clear and solid and aware of love. In the space I could hear my own heart. I could hear God. In the space was deep and profound peace. At the end of those twenty-four hours, as we gathered to break the silence in community, all I wanted was more. More silence. More rest. Since that day, I find I crave it. If it's been too long, the days too full, without silence and the solitude that accompanies it, I crave it like dark chocolate. My soul isn't satisfied with less.

The public years of Jesus' life pictured in the gospels are grounded in silence and solitude. Luke tells us that Jesus, full of the Spirit, was led into the solitude and silence of the wilderness for forty days. We're told he fasted. He was hungry. He was tempted. And at the end of these forty days, "Jesus returned to Galilee powerful in the Spirit."[9] Somehow fullness for even Jesus comes through the emptiness.

Again and again we read that Jesus withdrew to places of solitude, stepping away intentionally from his friends, from the crowds, from the demands of the hungry and sick: "in the morning, a great while before day, he rose and went out to a lonely place."[10] This was the rhythm of Jesus' life. The connection with his Father, the fullness that comes in emptiness, is restored for Jesus and for us in the place of rest.

Richard Foster describes this practice of silence—because it must be practiced and planned intentionally (it never just happens)—as "the stilling of what the old writers called 'creaturely activity.' This means not so much a silence of words as a silence of our grasping, manipulative control of people and situations. It means standing firm against our codependent drives to control everyone and fix everything. This agitated creaturely activity hinders the work of God in us. In *silencio*, therefore, we still every motion that is not rooted in God. We become quiet, hushed, motionless, until we are finally centered."[11]

In silence we allow all our baggage to be set aside, all our creaturely activity to be stripped away, so that we can simply be the created enjoying the presence of a joyful creator.

PRACTICING THE PRESENCE

In this prayer of quiet, this prayer of being still with no words, the activity of our minds is stilled and our spirits are awakened. The prayer of quiet is a prayer of listening and more. It is contemplation of the one who loves us, the experience of being loved. It is the pondering of Mary, who when told by an angel she would give birth to the Messiah, pondered all these things in her heart, holding them in trust, holding the treasure within her. We hold this same treasure within, the life of God. And we become aware of this life, of his presence in and around us, in the stillness. "Settle yourself in solitude," wrote Teresa of Avila, "and you will come upon him in yourself."[12]

The goal of this practice of presence, this contemplative prayer, is deepening connection with God. Julian of Norwich wrote, "The whole reason why we pray is to be united into the vision and contemplation of the one to whom we pray."[13] This union we seek is a deeper knowing, and we truly know only what we have experienced. The rest, the silence, the solitude, the waiting and contemplating, all open the door to an experience of his presence around and in us. In God's presence we come to know who he is and who we are. We move far beyond cognitive assent to the idea that God is loving and that we are loved. We "taste and see that the LORD is good."[14] We know it because we have tasted, touched, seen; we have experienced it.

Brother Lawrence, a simple Carmelite monk who worked in a monastery kitchen scouring pots, learned to practice the presence of God in the everyday. Many sought his wisdom and counsel to learn how to enter into this practice. His counsel was simple and always much the same. "We must know before we can love. In order to know God, we must often think of him; and when we come to love Him, we shall then also think of Him even more for our heart will be with our treasure."[15]

HOLDING THE SPACE

How does this practice become, well . . . something we can actually practice in our daily lives? How do we hold space for rest, silence, solitude, contemplation? Because I can turn that into a to-do list in a hot minute. And the to-doing is not the point. So how, in the midst of all we have to do in a day, do we find the rhythm of retreat to restore?

1. *Find your own rhythm.* There is no formula. In fact, formulas are the exact opposite of what we're talking about. What works for me probably won't work for you. And what works for me changes, as the seasons of my life change. So in a few moments of quiet, ask, "What does this look like in this season of my life?" Wait. Listen. What comes to mind? It might be a few moments of secluded quiet in the morning. Or evening. Or in the car. Or while you run. It might be your first silent retreat. It might be something you've never even thought of. But whatever comes to mind as you listen, try it. Experiment with it. Take a small step into the quiet. See how it feels. Keep listening. And keep going. The rhythm that's right for you will begin to emerge.

2. *Pull out your calendar.* You may need to schedule a time for silence and solitude if you're taking more than five or ten minutes. Consider it a date with yourself for yourself. Block out a morning, a day, or a weekend or more. Get intentional, and see what happens.

3. *Create your own sacred space.* You may need to set aside a space in your home that feels restful and peaceful to you. Pick a comfy chair. Light a candle. Have your favorite books or a journal nearby. Or maybe you need to leave your home and find a quiet spot in a park or place of beauty. What kind of space feels safe, peaceful, connected to you?

4. *Practice holy rest.* Take a nap.

5. *Take a walk alone and gaze upon beauty.* Contemplating beauty in nature, in art, in any form can help us contemplate the beauty of God.

6. *Things keep distracting you?* All the things I need to do tend to become louder when I get quiet. As things come to mind, jot them down on a sheet of paper or in your phone. Then release them, knowing you can come back to them later.

7. *Turn off the podcasts, music, YouTube videos, television.* Let your space get quiet and turn your thoughts toward God as you cook, clean, and do basic tasks around the house. Practice God's presence in the mundane moments of life.

8. *Take one small step.* A rhythm of rest, silence, and solitude is formed one practice at a time as sacred space opens in your soul. In the words of Richard Foster:

> Solitude is more a state of mind and heart than it is a place. There is a solitude of the heart that can be maintained at all times. Crowds, or the lack of them, have little to do with this inward attentiveness. It is quite possible to be a desert hermit and never experience solitude. But if we possess inward solitude we do not fear being alone, for we know that we are not alone. Neither do we fear being with others, for they do not control us. In the midst of noise and confusion we are settled into a deep inner silence. Whether alone or among people, we always carry with us a portable sanctuary of the heart.[16]

DEEPER (IN)

> Understand—through the stillness,
> Act—out of the stillness,
> Conquer—in the stillness.
>   —Dag Hammarskjold[17]

Sitting in Silence

Select a quiet space that feels safe and sacred to you where you can have at least ten minutes of uninterrupted time alone in silence. Leave your phone in another room or turn it off. Set a journal or piece of paper next to you so you can jot down things that come to mind—the distractions, the to-dos, and the thoughts that come as you listen.

Settle into your space taking a few deep breaths in and out. Lift a simple prayer. Something like, "Please settle my thoughts, my emotions, my body into peace. Help me to be still. God, I welcome your presence." Now be still. Wait. What do you sense? What thoughts come? Write them all down as they come. Don't worry about figuring out if they make sense or if they are God thoughts. Capture them all as they come. Stay quiet. Gaze on beauty around you. Turn your thoughts back toward God as many times as you need to. For ten full minutes.

When your time is up, reflect and write a bit about how this experience felt. What was hard? What, if anything, felt good about it? What were you aware of in the silence?

Now, review the things you wrote in your time of stillness. Gather your to-dos. Then look for things you wrote that feel like they have life on them. What are you hearing from your heart? What are you hearing from God? Ponder these in your heart.

Experiment with longer increments of time. Maybe try twenty minutes or thirty. Give yourself lots of grace as you go. Silence and solitude are called disciplines for a reason. You're building new muscle as you practice.

Moving in Silence

Some people find sitting still nearly impossible. They are made to move. Does that sound like you? If so, take a walk in silence. Pick a place that's not crowded or loud. Maybe a park or wooded area or a museum.

As you begin, ask God to quiet your mind and center your thoughts on him. What do you notice as you walk? What thoughts come to mind? Release distractions as they come and return your focus to Jesus. What do you hear from him? When you're done walking, spend a few minutes journaling about your experience.

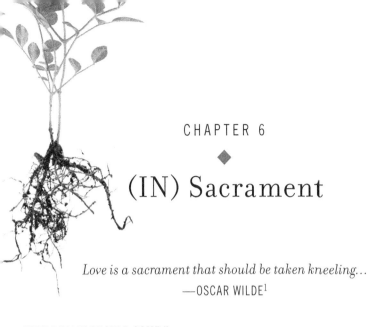

CHAPTER 6

◆

(IN) Sacrament

Love is a sacrament that should be taken kneeling...
—OSCAR WILDE[1]

"YOU REALLY SHOULD COME."

Some friends who knew Leanne Payne and her ministry suggested (strongly) that I come to a Ministries of Pastoral Care conference. I knew they were right. My on-again, off-again relationship with a man struggling with his sexual identity was off again. He had ended it, and I was devastated. I needed healing. Perhaps even more, I needed understanding. Why had I been so attracted to a man so ungrounded in his own identity? My sense of self had no deep roots, no inner stability. I desperately wanted a man to choose me so I would know I was loved, worthy, chosen, enough. And this man who was gentle, sensitive, who didn't yell like my father—this kind of man felt safe to me. But in choosing this man, I chose someone unable to choose me. And my deepest fear of being unchosen had been realized. I had woven a very tangled web, and I needed help to untangle it.

Without knowing anything really about the conference, I registered, bought a plane ticket, and flew across the country to Loyola University in California. My friends, who were part of the conference team that week, were completely shocked that I came. I was, too. Spontaneity and trying new things all by myself were way outside my comfort zone. But I was desperate, and desperation is fertile ground for healing.

So many amazing, healing things happened that week. My sense of being—the sense of solidness and well-being at my core—was restored. My identity as one beloved and chosen was strengthened. But the highlight came at the end.

Up to this point, my church experience had been: no church, charismatic church, and mainline evangelical church. I had never experienced a liturgical communion service. In fact, I was a little suspect of them. Because Leanne came from the Episcopal tradition and knew the healing power of the sacraments, she ended her conferences with a full-on liturgical communion service. An Anglican priest in full vestments began the service, and I began to weep uncontrollably. I tried to stop. I couldn't.

I had no idea why I was crying. It was a communion service, for heaven's sake, with a guy dressed in robes and a bunch of rote prayers. (Hearing any bias?) What was the big deal? With tears running down my face, I asked the Lord why I was crying. The response came: "Susan, I am restoring to you your Christian heritage." The prayers prayed for centuries by millions of believers around the world in a moment became my prayers. And I had a profound sense, a sense I could feel deep within, that I was being grafted into a larger body in a way I had never before experienced. And with this sense of (IN) came the knowing that I was not alone. I was a part of Jesus and his body. I was a part of something lasting and solid and true. And this knowing filled the emptiness, the sense of aloneness and isolation I'd felt all my life.

I was surprised to discover that I loved liturgy and the sense of rootedness I experienced praying these prayers. With time, I've realized sacraments of bread and wine and water are changing me. Because in some way, a way I'll never fully grasp, these sacraments take me (IN). Henri Nouwen expresses it well:

> Sacraments are very specific events in which God touches us through creation and transforms us into living

Christs. The two main sacraments are baptism and the Eucharist. In baptism water is the way to transformation. In the Eucharist it is bread and wine. The most ordinary things in life—water, bread, and wine—become the sacred way by which God comes to us. These sacraments are actual events. Water, bread, and wine are not simple reminders of God's love; they bring God to us. In baptism we are set free from the slavery of sin and dressed with Christ. In the Eucharist, Christ himself becomes our food and drink.[2]

Somehow, these symbols and prayers, held by followers of Jesus for centuries, have power to touch and shape and form me. They open encounter with an abstract Jesus in a way that makes him concrete, that makes his body real. He is touchable, smellable, see-able. And I, in my humanness, need desperately to touch and taste and see and join with something bigger than myself.

BREAD

The Israelites were grumbling.[3] Freed from slavery in Egypt, now on the other side of the Red Sea, there was only desert ahead. They were hungry and uncertain. And the familiarity of reliable meals in Egypt was feeling very appealing. After witnessing epic, prophetic plagues in Egypt that finally caused Pharaoh to free them from slavery . . . after walking between walls of water through the Red Sea . . . after all this, they anticipated only starvation. Surely, living as slaves was better than dying in the desert.

It would be easy to think they were being ridiculous. Really, how could they not believe and trust after seeing all that? But I'm just like them. Maybe you are, too. Because I forget all the time. I forget every five minutes that God is ahead of me and behind me, and that it is all his to do. I need to be reminded.

"Then the LORD said to Moses, 'I will rain down bread from heaven for you.'" Imagine that. Bread covering the ground like dew. Every morning. For forty years. Every day, God provided food for them. The bread that tasted like honey came in the morning for them to gather, then melted away in the sun. The quail came in the evening. Every day they had food as a reminder of the One who provided for them. It was all grace, this food. They didn't work for it. They simply received it and were sustained by it.

The LORD said to Moses, "I have heard the grumbling of the Israelites. Tell them, 'At twilight you will eat meat, and in the morning you will be filled with bread. Then you will know that I am the LORD your God.'"

"Then you will know." The point of the bread is the knowing and the remembering. "Then you will know that I am the LORD your God." The one who does for you what you cannot do for yourself. The one who sustains you wherever I lead you. Even in the desert. Remember every day who I am for you, and with you. I am the Lord who brought you out of slavery, into freedom.

I AM THE BREAD

"I am the bread of life." Jesus identified himself as bread. And this lost him some followers. Because what he was saying was pretty outrageous.

> Your ancestors ate the manna in the wilderness, yet they died. But here is the bread that comes down from heaven, which anyone may eat and not die. I am the living bread that came down from heaven. Whoever eats this bread will live forever. This bread is my flesh, which I will give for the life of the world. . . .
>
> Whoever eats my flesh and drinks my blood remains in me, and I in them. Just as the living Father sent me and I live because of the Father, so the one who feeds on me

will live because of me. This is the bread that came down from heaven.[4]

Remaining. Something about eating and drinking, taking Jesus in, helps us to remain, to stay connected. How can this be, this eating flesh and drinking blood? This kind of talk is offensive. It sounds cannibalistic. What can Jesus mean?

In the last week of Jesus' life, he prepared to celebrate the Passover with his friends. He knew he was headed to his death. He'd said this repeatedly to his friends. And now he showed them the full extent of his love:

> And he took bread, gave thanks and broke it, and gave it to them, saying, "This is my body given for you; do this in remembrance of me." In the same way, after the supper he took the cup, saying, "This cup is the new covenant in my blood, which is poured out for you."[5]

Jesus gives us bread and wine, from an ancient feast that marks freedom, to become flesh and blood for us in a way we can remember and celebrate. He becomes manna for us. Daily bread. This food and drink, this remembrance, helps us remain connected to the vine. Jesus takes the common things and makes them channels of life and freedom. Channels of his presence. A presence we can literally take into us.

"I am the living bread that came down from heaven. Whoever eats this bread will live forever." I think Jesus was making abstract truth a very present reality, a sacramental reality. We must take Jesus in. Every day. As he is (IN) us, we must continue to take him (IN). Through Word and Spirit. Through communion—common bread and wine made holy by prayer and purpose. Not just reminding us of what Jesus did, but becoming life in us. Richard Foster puts it this way: "As C. S. Lewis suggested, the command is 'to Take, eat; not Take, understand.'

Mystery invites us to participate in something that is beyond us, yet present to us. Present to all our senses."[6]

This bread thing is a big deal. I think we Protestants tend to make the whole thing an exercise in symbolism—a polite remembering of what Jesus did, clean and sterile. We tear off a piece of bread or (God forbid) take a wafer, and think thoughts about what Jesus did for us in his life and sacrifice. And that's all good, as far as it goes. But there's more to be had here. Much more.

When something real—real bread, real wine—enters us, we encounter in a tangible way the real presence of Jesus. His body and blood present to us. This is an encounter with the body broken, the blood spilled, that is our healing. Our very life. We somehow actually participate in his body when we take the bread and the cup. How this happens is mystery. But this mystery moves our hearts from a position of out to a position of (IN). In communion we come again to remain, to live in union with Jesus. And this is the point. It is about our oneness with him, the one who is our healing, the one who is our life. "The Eucharist," says Richard Rohr, "becomes our ongoing touchstone through the Christian journey, a place we must keep going to in order to find our face, our name, our absolute identity, who we are in Christ, and thus who we are forever."[7]

Oneness, unity with Jesus, means that I am living united with him, spirit to Spirit. My spirit, my very being, breathing as one with the Spirit of God. The Spirit of God living in me, living through me. God in me. Me in God. This remembering is a returning to the place of union. It's called communion for a reason.

WATER

In the sense that communion is Jesus (IN) us, baptism—being dunked in or sprinkled with water—is us (IN) Jesus. About five minutes after I'd prayed and committed my life to following Jesus, my youth pastor told me I needed to be baptized. I'd been sprinkled as

a baby, which of course I didn't remember, but I was eager to seal
this new life in a way that was real and meaningful to me as an adult.
I immediately agreed, completely not knowing I was agreeing to be
submerged in water in front of the entire church. I assumed adults
were sprinkled like babies, because sprinkling was all I'd ever seen.
I was not prepared to be soaked head to toe. Honestly, I did not want
to stand in front of one hundred people with wet hair and mascara
running. I was an eighteen-year old girl, after all. But I'd said yes,
and there was no turning back.

The next Sunday I walked into the baptismal tub at the front of
the church. My youth pastor introduced me, then asked me to share
why I was being baptized. I wasn't prepared to speak, and I didn't
really have words yet to say much about the change in my life. But I
said something, and everyone nodded, smiled, and said "Amen" very
loudly. So I guess I'd said something that made sense. Next thing I
knew, I was under the water and up again.

The physical experience of being buried in water and raised up
from the water-grave embedded the death and resurrection of Jesus
in my soul. That physical experience was a spiritual encounter with
the truth that I was now new, risen in Christ. I can still almost feel
the water running off my face as I was pulled up into new life. Baptism was and is more than a symbol to me. It is a real experience of
very real grace and truth. And it stands in my spirit as a marker. I
have crossed over from death to life.

Jesus chose to be baptized. For even Jesus, something about
the water was important. And that something was about Spirit and
identity—a marking of truth. The giver of living water, the one who
walked on water, chose to go under the water.

As soon as Jesus was baptized, he went up out of the
water. At that moment heaven was opened, and he saw the
Spirit of God descending like a dove and alighting on him.

And a voice from heaven said, "This is my Son, whom I love; with him I am well pleased."[8]

We need markers in our lives, places to experience and remember what is true. We are washed. We are clean. We are new. We are, in Christ, the ones who are loved and with whom God is pleased. And from this new place, we enter into the new adventure of living more deeply rooted in love.

Every day, the invitation is new. Today, again, you're invited to remember who God is. Remember who you are. Turn again and take your place in what is true. You (IN) God. God (IN) you. In Him, normal jobs, normal days, normal encounters with family and neighbors, normal bread and wine and water, become more. They become opportunities for God to break in, for healing to break in, for his presence to come. And his presence changes everything.

WORD

We are back to bread again. But this time in a different form. It comes as word.

"Jesus answered, 'It is written: "Man shall not live on bread alone, but on every word that comes from the mouth of God."[9] It seems we are meant to take the word of God in, just as we take in bread. The daily bread that feeds and sustains spirit and soul as well as body. This is a living word, coming from the mouth of God to us, alive with meaning. It is alive because it comes from the one who is life and the source of all life. And apparently, we need this word just like we need food to live.

> In the beginning was the Word, and the Word was with God, and the Word was God. He was with God in the beginning. Through him all things were made; without him nothing was made that has been made. In him was life, and

that life was the light of all mankind. The light shines in the
darkness, and the darkness has not overcome it.[10]

These are John's words. The one Jesus loved. His best friend who
spent three years, day and night, with him. The one who laid against
Jesus' chest. John knows Jesus as the Word, the Word that is God.
The Word that is life and light. The Word that overcomes. The Word
through whom all that's been created was created. The Word through
whom you and I and everything exists.

This Word is not merely a word on a page. A written set of rules
or law or knowledge to be mastered by the mind. This Word is alive,
expansive, before time, through time. This Word is still speaking,
still bringing life and light, still overcoming, still creating in and
through you and me as we hear and respond. And this Word, as we
listen and hear and respond, helps us remain.

> You are already clean because of the word I have spoken
> to you. Remain in me, as I also remain in you. No branch
> can bear fruit by itself; it must remain in the vine. Neither
> can you bear fruit unless you remain in me.[11]

By the word spoken by the Word, we are already clean. Somehow,
as we abide, as we remain in the vine, his words restore with life and
light. As we hear from Jesus what is true about God and true about
us, we come to know and experience this truth that transforms. We
become more fully ourselves. We become fruitful.

Perhaps the words of the Bible have not felt like life to you. Perhaps they've been used to bully. Perhaps you've experienced them
as law, rules to be followed. But you're invited to something more.
You're invited to engage with the written Word as sacrament, a means
of connecting with God and receiving grace. You're invited to listen
and hear what God is speaking to you for your life today. Because if

you're like me, you need life and light and grace and truth today. Like right now. Without it, we can't remain.

The words of the Hebrew and Christian Scriptures are filled with poetry and story and wisdom and song. And sometimes much of the beauty is lost as theologians and preachers pull verses apart and put them back together to make meaning for us. As we come simply to receive the words, to listen with our hearts and minds, to let them form us, shape us, challenge us, the meaning is made (IN) us. The living Word speaks. Light shines. We are washed and made clean. As we prayerfully read Scripture, as we prayerfully hear timeless verses read, we encounter the One who is the Word. And the encounter is the point.

A SACRAMENTAL LIFE

Maybe all this talk about sacraments is making you itchy. Maybe it feels churchy, and that has some baggage for you. And that's OK. I felt the same way. Hang with me. Let's make this bigger.

A sacramental life is a symbolic life. We as humans are symbolic beings. We make meaning from the things we see around us all the time. We find meaning within the larger story of our lives and communities. So look around. Listen. Smell. Taste. Touch. How do the most ordinary things you encounter every day remind you of grace? Be a meaning-maker.

The smell of bread baking. The giggle of a baby. The colors of spring. The sound of wind in the trees. The homeless person you pass. Music drifting from the neighbor's yard. Water gurgling in a stream. The warmth of sunshine against your skin. The smell of rain. The bittersweetness of dark chocolate. The sound of glasses clinking together. The softness of puppies. The warm, sudsy, scented water in a bath. A touch from your child or partner or friend. How does it speak of beauty and dignity and life? How does it bring God present to you?

What if it's all holy? A sacramental life sees the holy everywhere. Everything speaks. The beauty of creation—holy. The dignity of humans, made in the likeness of God—all holy. Dividers come down as we live in the common union of life in God and God in us.

Sacrament is incarnational grace, God present with us now, today, in this moment, in ways we can see, taste, touch, smell. Bread, wine, water, word—all bring us to God and bring God to us. In sacrament we remember. In sacrament we remain.

History, tradition, sacred texts, the symbols and words of liturgy—all root us in a broader, shared experience. A narrative that grounds us in what we share, what we have in common. There's a reason the prayer book used by many liturgical churches is called the Book of Common Prayer. We share these prayers with those who pray beside us and with all who've prayed these prayers across time and space.

Shauna Niequist writes beautifully about this: "It's so meaningful to me to balance the relative youth of my tradition with the deep rootedness of the Catholic church, or the liturgy, or the Book of Common Prayer. I like feeling connected to something durable and beautiful, something that has endured centuries."[12]

My love for sacrament has grown since my first encounter with a liturgical communion service. I'm grateful that my husband and I are now part of a worshipping community that is seeking to hold different expressions of worship together—traditional, contemporary, social, liturgical, spontaneous. This body is bringing streams together that normally don't flow in one place. It feels alive to me, rooted, grounded, yet never stagnant, always flowing. At the end of every service, we sing a doxology, written as part of two hymns in 1674 by Thomas Ken:

> Praise God, from whom all blessings flow;
> Praise Him, all creatures here below;
> Praise Him above, ye heavenly host;
> Praise Father, Son, and Holy Ghost. Amen.

Voices raise in harmony, *a capella*, singing the words sung by millions across time. You'd think it might get old, singing this old song every Sunday. But it is as if the saints through the ages and the saints in the room are joined in a common expression of worship. I experience deep connection again with God, with those beside me, and with all those who've gone before me. And this connection through sacrament opens the way, said C.S. Lewis, to the real:

> What God is in Himself, how He is to be conceived by philosophers, retreats continually from our knowledge. The elaborate word-pictures which accompany religion and look each so solid while they last, turn out to be only shadows. It is religion itself—prayer and sacrament and repentance and adoration—which is here in the long run, our sole avenue to the real.[13]

DEEPER (IN)

Bread and Wine

The communion service is perhaps the most celebrated liturgical prayer. It unites elements of confession, forgiveness, remembrance, and celebration. And it includes what is perhaps the most famous prayer taught by Jesus to his followers, known as the Lord's Prayer. For this experience, you'll need some wine or juice, and a piece of bread or cracker. Find a quiet spot and take a few moments of silence. Invite Holy Spirit to guide this time. Then read these words slowly, prayerfully, out loud:

> The Lord Jesus, on the night he was betrayed, took bread, and when he had given thanks, he broke it and said, "This is my body, which is for you; do this in remembrance of me." In the same way, after supper he took the cup, saying, "This cup is the new covenant in my blood; do this, whenever you drink it, in remembrance of me." For whenever you eat this bread and drink this cup, you proclaim the Lord's death until he comes.[14]

Now take a bite of bread or cracker. Chew slowly. Taste it. Feel it as you swallow. Then take a drink of wine or juice. Hold it in your mouth for a minute, tasting it, then swallowing. How do you experience Jesus' death and life as you eat and drink?

Now slowly pray these words out loud. Listen to the words as you pray:

> Our Father in heaven,
> hallowed be your name,
> your kingdom come,
> your will be done,

on earth as it is in heaven.

Give us today our daily bread.

And forgive us our debts,

  as we also have forgiven our debtors.

And lead us not into temptation,

but deliver us from the evil one.[15]

How is the living Word speaking to you today? What is highlighted to you? What feels important for today? Do you feel an invitation to respond in some way? Pray, write, journal, paint, or draw about your thoughts and response.

As an alternative, rather than reading the communion passage, try listening. BibleGateway.com and other online Bible resources offer audio recordings of Scripture. As you take your bread and wine, listen to the words of Jesus in Matthew 26:17–30.

◆

CHAPTER 7

(IN) Spirit

I don't want my life to be explainable
without the Holy Spirit.
—FRANCIS CHAN[1]

I'D INVITED AUTHOR AND theologian Jack Deere to come to Cincinnati as the featured speaker for a small conference on healing. Jack's books had been formative for me in my journey in the Spirit. After one of his sessions, Jack took a few moments to listen, asking God what he wanted to do in our ministry time, then shared with us a few things he'd heard—including the thought that God wanted to heal allergies.

The prayer teams came to the front, and people were invited to come to a team for prayer. I immediately noticed a young boy making a beeline toward me with a huge smile on his face. He was followed closely by his two parents. They were not smiling; they looked worried. I got down on my knees, eye to eye with the boy, and asked what he wanted us to ask Jesus for. He replied, "I'm allergic to peanuts and I want to eat peanut butter." This little boy was responding in trust to the word Jack had given. And inside, honestly, my response was "Crap." My silent, very quick conversation with God went something like this: "God, nothing in me believes you'll do this. And I'm not OK with this little boy being disappointed. So I need you to show up now." This is not, for the record, a faith-filled prayer.

With a big smile on my face (because this little boy didn't need to see my personal crisis), I began to pray. Honestly, it felt like my words fell to the floor. I felt no sense of power or God's presence. I prayed a little more, blessing his body to receive peanuts, asking God to reverse the allergic reactions in his body. Then I ran out of things to pray, so I stopped. It felt like absolutely nothing was happening. I said "Amen." His father said, "Is that all?" Yes, that was all. Clearly he was disappointed, but that little boy wasn't.

I heard the rest of the story when they called me from the doctor's office. When Grant got back to his seat, he asked his parents to be tested again. Now you see why his parents looked worried: They didn't want their little boy to be disappointed either. Grant had a life-threatening peanut allergy. This was a very big deal for all of them. But they agreed and took Grant to be tested. After a series of tests, I got the call. No allergy. Grant was eating his first spoonful of peanut butter.

My super-holy response was, "No way! Seriously?" I could barely hold back the tears until I was off the phone. Clearly, God had shown up. He had not disappointed Grant. And it had nothing to do with me, except I was present as a conduit, open to the flow of the presence of God to connect with a little boy. Grant's healing was the beginning of a larger healing in his family, grounding them again in the love of God. And what's better than being a small part of the bigger story God is writing all around us?

We are invited every day by Spirit, in Spirit, to participate in the generous love of God. To add our yes and amen to what God is already doing in and around us. To live in the flow of healing mercy.

THE ULTIMATE (IN)

The disciples were really upset. They had just shared the Passover meal with Jesus, and he had given them a new commandment to love one another, just as he loved them. They weren't upset about the love;

it was the next part. Jesus told them they needed to know this new commandment because he was going away, somewhere they could not follow, to prepare a place for them. They weren't fully getting it. They had a lot of questions. It was all sounding bad. The one they loved, the one they'd given up everything to follow, was leaving. And they were being left behind.

> If you love me, keep my commands. And I will ask the Father, and he will give you another advocate to help you and be with you forever—the Spirit of truth. The world cannot accept him, because it neither sees him nor knows him. But you know him, for he lives with you and will be in you. I will not leave you as orphans; I will come to you. Before long, the world will not see me anymore, but you will see me. Because I live, you also will live. On that day you will realize that I am in my Father, and you are in me, and I am in you. Whoever has my commands and keeps them is the one who loves me. The one who loves me will be loved by my Father, and I too will love them and show myself to them.[2]

You are in me. I am in you. Just as Jesus is in the Father, the disciples will live in (IN)timate connection with Jesus because he will send Holy Spirit. Jesus begins to tell them what it will mean to live (IN) him, to live in love, obeying this commandment, being his body on Earth when he is gone. Jesus added, "Anyone who loves me will obey my teaching. My Father will love them, and we will come to them and make our home with them."[3] In Spirit, the Father and son come to make their home in each of us. Father, Jesus, Spirit move (IN), literally. And as friends we become family—daughters and sons.

Is any of this sounding familiar? If so, it's because all this leads to abiding; Jesus goes on to talk about vines and branches—intimate, life-giving connection. Remember Chapter 2? This conversation about Holy Spirit between Jesus and his friends is in the context of abiding. The coming of Spirit. The one who will move in, live in, remain in us so that we can remain in him. And Jesus tells them this is better—even better than having him physically present with them.

> Rather, you are filled with grief because I have said these things. But very truly I tell you, it is for your good that I am going away. Unless I go away, the Advocate will not come to you; but if I go, I will send him to you. . . .
>
> I have much more to say to you, more than you can now bear. But when he, the Spirit of truth, comes, he will guide you into all the truth. He will not speak on his own; he will speak only what he hears, and he will tell you what is yet to come. He will glorify me because it is from me that he will receive what he will make known to you. All that belongs to the Father is mine. That is why I said the Spirit will receive from me what he will make known to you.[4]

This is big. In fact, this is everything. Spirit will come. To advocate. To speak. To guide. To glorify. To make known. To take what belongs to the Father and to Jesus, and to make it known to us. Father, Jesus, Spirit in us. The fullness, the presence, the person of God within. This is the ultimate (IN). And this makes living rooted, grounded, remaining possible. This makes joy and fruitfulness possible. This makes everything possible.

"It is a light within which illumines the face of God and casts new shadows and new glories upon our faces," wrote Quaker Thomas Kelly. "It is a seed stirring to life if we do not choke it. It is the Shekinah of the soul, the Presence in the midst. Here is the slumbering Christ, stirring to be awakened, to become the soul we clothe in earthly form and action. And he is within us all."[5]

BEING FILLED

It looked, well, a little crazy. Because sometimes when the God of the universe shows up, it's like that.

> When the day of Pentecost came, they were all together in one place. Suddenly a sound like the blowing of a violent wind came from heaven and filled the whole house where they were sitting. They saw what seemed to be tongues of fire that separated and came to rest on each of them. All of them were filled with the Holy Spirit and began to speak in other tongues as the Spirit enabled them.[6]

Violent wind. Fire. People thought the disciples were drunk. They were speaking in the languages of all the people gathered for the feast of Pentecost, languages they didn't know. Peter stood up and gave his first sermon—and the church exploded. Thousands became followers of Jesus that day. The Spirit of Jesus was unleashed in the world.

Jesus gives an amazing gift: the gift of Spirit, available to all. This is a gift that keeps on giving. The apostle Paul writes years later to the believers in Ephesus that they are to be continually filled with the Spirit. "Do not get drunk on wine, which leads to debauchery. Instead, be filled with the Spirit, speaking to one another with psalms, hymns, and songs from the Spirit."[7] The verb "be filled" is progressive, meaning to be being filled not once, but again and again. This world takes a lot out of us. And it seems, like a tire, we have a slow leak. We need a refill.

Picture a snow globe. The globe contains liquid and "snow." As it sits on your shelf, before you shake it, it is full of snow. You just can't see it yet. When you shake the globe, it fills with the snow. There's no more or less snow in it than there was when it sat on your shelf. But now the globe is full of snow in a way it wasn't before. Shaking the globe activates the snow.

In the same way, as we are (IN) God and God is (IN) us, we are full of Holy Spirit. And yet when we ask to be filled and refilled, Spirit in us is activated and we are filled in a more visible, tangible way, a way that is obvious to us and to the world. And the fruit of the filling is union, loving connection with God with ourselves and with others—because what fills us is the life and love, the fullness of Jesus.

MORE LOVE, MORE POWER

I was new at following Jesus and I had a lot of questions. About two weeks into this new journey, I walked up to my pastor with my Bible open. I had read all the Gospels for the first time. In fact, I'd read from Matthew to Romans at this point. I was enthralled with Jesus. I pointed to a few passages, passages about healing and hearing God and that kind of thing, and asked, "When do we get to do it?" I saw a lot of people who really loved God, but I didn't see anyone doing the stuff Jesus did every day of his life on Earth. Reading the Bible for the first time, it was clear to me that as Jesus-followers, we got to do this stuff. My pastor looked at me kindly and responded humbly, "Honestly, Susan, I just don't know."

My question, and his answer, launched me on a mission. It seemed clear to me that I was invited to live like Jesus. And it was very clear that Jesus lived a supernatural life fueled by Holy Spirit. No one had tried to tell me yet that this kind of thing doesn't happen anymore. This is what I'd signed up for. I just couldn't find anyone living this kind of life.

I had been following Jesus for about six weeks when I arrived at Vanderbilt. My new friends took me under their more seasoned wings, promising to show me how to do this new Jesus thing. I was swept into multiple college fellowship groups and Bible studies. I learned so much that was good, and I'm grateful for the grounding I received. But nothing in this traditional Christian discipleship track spoke to the supernatural. It was mostly about me doing a lot of right things with God's help. And it was mostly about reading, knowing, studying, memorizing Scripture. The Trinity looked more like Father, Son, Holy Bible. The life of Spirit was missing.

I found others who were searching, asking the same questions. But Donna was the first person I met who could talk about Holy Spirit like she knew him. I'd graduated and started my first job in the crazy little marketing research firm. Donna was part of the team. She was married to a Pentecostal pastor. As we talked one day in her office, me asking all my questions, she started talking about the Spirit in a way that made sense to me. "Susan, you just ask him to fill you. We could pray for you for that, but it would be loud, and you'd be really uncomfortable. So why don't you just go home tonight and ask him to fill you?" Seriously? It's that easy? And it doesn't have to be all loud and awkward and dramatic?

So I did. I went home, lit a candle (because a little atmosphere never hurts), and asked. "Holy Spirit, I want all you have for me. Please fill me." Short. Simple. And as I waited, I was aware of a quiet warmth within enlarging in my belly, in my heart, a sense of life, joy, filling. Then an overwhelming sense of love. I was lying down now, feeling the weight of what I can only describe as warm love overtaking me. It felt thick inside, like the joy and love had substance. I didn't want it to end. When I finally got up, what had felt like minutes had been well over an hour. I felt more alive than I'd ever felt before. And I knew love in a way I'd never known it before—because it went from being a thought to an experience.

Mathematician and scientist Blaise Pascal encountered this same Spirit on November 23, 1654. He sewed this note into the lining of his coat and carried it with him for the rest of his life:

Fire. God of Abraham, the God of Isaac, the God of Jacob, not of the philosophers and scholars. Certainty. Certainty, heartfelt joy, peace. God of Jesus Christ. Joy, joy, joy, oceans of joy![8]

WHERE HEAVEN AND EARTH MEET

It's tempting to compare and evaluate experiences—to base our beliefs on what we have or haven't experienced. And to completely dismiss anything that's a little, well, weird. But here's the thing: God-encounters are unique to each of our stories and have been unique throughout history. The Desert Fathers, the apostle John, mystics like Julian of Norwich and Madam Guyon, John Wesley, Jonathan Edwards, Smith Wigglesworth, Kathryn Kuhlman, John Wimber, Heidi Baker, Randy Clark—women and men throughout history have encountered God in ways that are "similarly different." When the presence of an infinite God connects with a finite human body, all kinds of things can happen. The aim is not a particular kind of experience; it is an encounter with God that grounds us in his love and opens the way to a deeper knowing. Opens the way to flow. We are invited to live with an awareness of God's presence. And that is all gift.

A contemplative, connected life is an experiential life, an (IN) life. It is a life of Spirit, and it will look different for each of us. (Trying to have an experience just like someone else's experience is a recipe for weird.) Experiential knowing, an awareness of God's presence in and around us, happens in quiet moments and loud: As we experience God present with us as we read, pray, wash dishes, stare into the eyes of a new baby, take a walk in the woods—or, as we see God heal a peanut allergy. In these moments, the distance between the physical world and spiritual things, we become aware that God is, indeed, with us. And when this happens, it is Spirit.

Maybe you're like me. Maybe you've seen excesses and abuses and craziness connected with Holy Spirit. Maybe you've been hurt or disappointed. Maybe you've decided this whole thing just isn't for you. I don't blame you. I get it. Holy Spirit is abused and misrepresented.

People focus on the power—and there *is* power. But the source of the power is love, and the point of the power is knowing this love. Making love visible to us and to others. The miracles of Jesus, the power of his Spirit, are demonstrations, visible signs to the world, like snow in the globe, of the love and nature of Jesus. If we miss the love, we miss it all.

> If I speak in the tongues of men or of angels, but do not have love, I am only a resounding gong or a clanging cymbal. If I have the gift of prophecy and can fathom all mysteries and all knowledge, and if I have a faith that can move mountains, but do not have love, I am nothing. If I give all I possess to the poor and give over my body to hardship that I may boast, but do not have love, I gain nothing.
>
> Love is patient, love is kind. It does not envy, it does not boast, it is not proud. It does not dishonor others, it is not self-seeking, it is not easily angered, it keeps no record of wrongs. Love does not delight in evil but rejoices with the truth. It always protects, always trusts, always hopes, always perseveres.
>
> Love never fails.[9]

I forget this all the time. I need to be reminded every five minutes (or less). This God who is love is not just with me. He is (IN) me. The One who raised the dead, healed the sick, washed dirty feet, and loved the unlovable, this One lives in me. His love is living and active. His love never fails.

Theologian N. T. Wright states, "Those in whom the Spirit comes to live are God's new Temple. They are, individually and corporately, places where heaven and earth meet."[10] And when heaven meets Earth, good news breaks out all over the place.

When Jesus went public with his ministry, he stood in the temple and read a prophetic scripture from the book of Isaiah—and told them this prophecy was being fulfilled in their presence:

The Spirit of the Lord is on me,

　because he has anointed me

　to proclaim good news to the poor.

He has sent me to proclaim freedom for the prisoners

　and recovery of sight for the blind,

　to set the oppressed free,

　to proclaim the year of the Lord's favor.[11]

This is what Spirit life looks like. What love looks like. It looks like good news, like the favor of God showing up in person, with skin on. The hungry are fed. The blind see, literally and figuratively. Those oppressed and imprisoned are set free. When we live Spirit-filled, this is what our lives look like. We embody the supernatural love that can heal the world.

UNION

This is deep mystery. The fullness of a three-in-one God living in us. And us—you and me—somehow living in this very God. And yet, this seems to be the point. Our lonely, isolated hearts need connection. We were made for this connection. If we stay still long enough, if we stop numbing with media and food and sex and alcohol, we feel the emptiness within and around us. And it feels dark and terrible. Father and Jesus come, as Spirit, to meet us in the aloneness to fill the emptiness. Restored to connection with the life source of the vine, the branch receives all it needs to thrive.

"The same Spirit," wrote Andrew Murray, "which dwelt and still dwells in the Son, becomes the life of the believer; in the unity of that one Spirit, and the fellowship of the same life which is in Christ, he is one with Him. As between the vine and branch, it is a life-union that makes them one."[12] This union is the place of true knowing, because in this union we come to know by experience the love of God. As we know the One who is love, we know ourselves as beloved. The Spirit gives power to know this love, not as an abstract idea or words on a page, but as reality. And this reality in us is the full measure of the fullness of God, doing in and through us immeasurably more than we can imagine. And so we find ourselves back where we began:

> I pray that out of his glorious riches he may strengthen you with power through his Spirit in your inner being, so that Christ may dwell in your hearts through faith. And I pray that you, being rooted and established in love, may have power, together with all the Lord's holy people, to grasp how wide and long and high and deep is the love of Christ, and to know this love that surpasses knowledge—that you may be filled to the measure of all the fullness of God.
>
> Now to him who is able to do immeasurably more than all we ask or imagine, according to his power that is at work within us, to him be glory in the church and in Christ Jesus throughout all generations, for ever and ever! Amen.[13]

DEEPER (IN)

> May the God of hope fill you with all joy and peace as
> you trust in him, so that you may overflow with hope by the
> power of the Holy Spirit.[14]

Holy Spirit is moving with intention in and around us all the time. We're invited to become active participants, to become a part of what he's already doing. This is where the best adventures begin.

So how do we experience more of this fullness, more of this love, more of this power? How do we live a more connected life with God by the Spirit? I've found these three practices helpful. Consider each and pick the one that stirs something in you. The one stirring is Holy Spirit.

Connect with the Spirit

One of the things Jesus said Holy Spirit would do was speak. He would share with us what we needed to know. You can talk with him just like you talk with Jesus and the Father. Ask him questions. Listen. Write what you hear in response. Develop an interior life of listening to the voice of Holy Spirit within.

Release Any Baggage or Offenses with Holy Spirit

What do you believe about Holy Spirit that isn't true? How have you limited his fullness and presence in your life? Be honest. If you're ready, ask Holy Spirit to fill or refill you. Ask him to release in you the love, joy, peace, patience, kindness, goodness, gentleness, self-control you need.

Take a Risk

John Wimber, founder of the Vineyard movement, used to say that faith is a four-letter word: *risk*. This is where the adventure begins. Everybody gets to play. We get to do the stuff Jesus did. Ask Holy Spirit to move in and through your life in new ways as you embody the Spirit of Jesus on the planet. How does he want to bring heaven to Earth through you today?

CHAPTER 8

◆

(IN) Grace

For me, every hour is grace.[1]
—ELIE WIESEL

IT WAS MAY 1988. For the first time in history, the US government was trying to send a health alert to every US household by mail. It was part of a three-week media campaign designed to inform Americans about AIDS. Fear was driving the reactions to a growing health crisis. I stood in my apartment reading the pamphlet. And as I read, a hook sunk into my heart. I literally felt a physical pain and tug in my chest. I thought of some of my best friends from high school who were gay and possibly at risk. Immediately, this was personal to me. This was about people I loved. Immediately and inexplicably, I felt compelled to respond in some way. I knew I had to do something. I knew Jesus wanted to do something. But I had no idea what.

For the next year, I was borderline-obsessive. I read all I could get my hands on to learn about HIV/AIDS. I searched in our city to see who was responding and how. I talked about it all the time, which made me a delight at parties. And I prayed—by which I mean, mostly listened. A lot. In that year, a plan began to form. I felt it was God's plan. I would call churches around the city together to serve people with HIV/AIDS. To just show up and serve, no strings attached. We would love the people that few were loving at that time. We would love the gay community and people living and dying with AIDS.

Jesus seemed to prefer to spend time with the outcasts, the people the religious leaders of his day excluded. If Jesus were walking around the streets of Cincinnati in 1988 (or today), he'd be hanging out with people with HIV/AIDS. He'd have dinner with them. Go to their homes. Wash their feet. We would do the same.

A year passed. I felt I knew who to call and what to do. I just didn't know when to do it. Periodically, I'd ask God: Is it time? Repeatedly, I'd hear, "No, not yet." So I was shocked the day I asked, sitting in my cubicle at work, and heard, "Yes, now." I took a deep breath, picked up the phone, and started calling.

Lloyd was the volunteer director at what was then called AIDS Volunteers of Cincinnati. He did not want to see me. Most AVOC volunteers were from the gay community and so was he. He didn't trust Christians, and I didn't expect him to. Why would he? Much of the Christian community had rejected the gay community and condemned people with AIDS. I would learn later, as we became friends, that he'd been rejected by his Christian family when he came out.

"No, really. We just want to serve. Please, can I meet with you?" He finally agreed to a short meeting. As I listened to his story and he listened to mine, the short meeting became about two hours and we became friends. By the time we finished, he'd asked me to be editor of their newsletter. More importantly, he called Caracole on our behalf, a residence for people with AIDS, and opened the door for us to serve there. I was stepping into the flow of Spirit. It was all grace.

One Saturday morning a month, our team would show up to Caracole. We brought homecooked meals and went to work. We would do whatever jobs needed to be done that day—scrubbing toilets, cleaning kitchens, dusting, yard work, painting. The first few visits, the residents kept their distance. Many of them, I would learn, had been bullied with a Bible by family and friends. Slowly they warmed to us, beginning to trust. And in the flow of grace, it happened.

"You people really are Christians. Just like in the Bible." One of the residents was talking to a volunteer. He'd been watching us. And slowly his preconceptions began to melt. He didn't have a great history with Christians, but he was experiencing something different. He was experiencing grace. His words undid me. He'd seen Jesus in us. Without a word, he'd encountered grace.

GRACE IS GIFT

Charis, the Greek word for grace, has several related meanings. It is unmerited, unqualified favor, blessing, and lovingkindness. It is power that strengthens and enables and saves. It is a gift (or gifts) from Holy Spirit.

This is the favor Mary received: "Greetings, you who are highly favored!"[2] The angel told Mary she would be overshadowed by Holy Spirit and conceive the Messiah, the one who would save and deliver. "Favored" (a form of *charis*) here can be translated "to make graceful," to make full of grace. Mary would be filled with grace to conceive by grace the one who is grace—the one who saves, heals, and delivers. Everything conceived, created as gift to the world, comes by grace. And we like Mary have been overshadowed by Holy Spirit, filled with grace and given gifts of grace much needed by the world.

> The Word became flesh and made his dwelling among us. We have seen his glory, the glory of the one and only Son, who came from the Father, full of grace and truth. . . .
>
> Out of his fullness we have all received grace in place of grace already given. For the law was given through Moses; grace and truth came through Jesus Christ. No one has ever seen God, but the one and only Son, who is himself God and is in closest relationship with the Father, has made him known.[3]

Jesus embodies grace and truth together, and in him, we receive grace upon grace. This gift has already been given. Before we do anything. Before we achieve, meet a standard, or keep the law (as if we could), we already have the gift. Brennan Manning writes, "Christianity is not primarily a moral code but a grace-laden mystery; it is not essentially a philosophy of love but a love affair; it is not keeping rules with clenched fists but receiving a gift with open hands."[4]

This gift is the remedy to our shame. As we live more firmly and deeply rooted and remaining in the love of God, receiving the gift, the atmosphere in and around us begins to shift from not enough to enough. Shame tells us we are what we've done or what's been done to us. We are too broken or bruised or used. The lies we've told, the damage we've done, the abuse we've endured, the abandonment, all leave us too dirty to ever be clean again. Shame is an unrelenting abuser. And grace comes to rescue us.

Shame and vulnerability researcher Dr. Brené Brown says shame is the intensely painful feeling that we are unworthy of love and belonging. She says it's the most primitive human emotion we all feel—and the one no one wants to talk about. Left to its own devices, shame can destroy lives.[5]

Shame is the destroyer Eve and Adam experienced in the garden. Open, naked, vulnerable connection with one another and with God was lost. This is the shame stuck like Crazy Glue to our humanity. The shame that sends us into hiding.

Shame says who you are is wrong. No matter what you do, you are not enough. But grace remembers who you really are and says you are enough. By gift. Not because you earned it. Not because you cleaned it up. Grace has nothing to do with what you do. It has everything to do with who you are, created, rooted, and established in the lovingkindness of God.

GRACE SAVES

So here, as they say, is the rub: If all this grace is gift, why don't I embody more grace for myself and for others? I still judge others. I still judge myself. I find my worth in what I do. I strive to meet impossible standards—mostly set by me, sometimes set by others. I fear being left out, left behind. I take the best seat, eat too much, laugh too little, worry a lot. It gets kind of ugly out here.

And it's precisely because of the ugly that I desperately need grace. Because grace saves, heals, restores, and recovers. Without grace, I am lost.

> But because of his great love for us, God, who is rich in mercy, made us alive with Christ even when we were dead in transgressions—it is by grace you have been saved. And God raised us up with Christ and seated us with him in the heavenly realms in Christ Jesus, in order that in the coming ages he might show the incomparable riches of his grace, expressed in his kindness to us in Christ Jesus. For it is by grace you have been saved, through faith—and this is not from yourselves, it is the gift of God—not by works, so that no one can boast.[6]

The word "save" here in Greek is *sozo*. In its truest essence, this word means "rescued." It's translated as "saved," "healed," and "delivered" in different places in the New Testament, because all these very big ideas are included in this one little word. By grace alone we are saved, healed, and rescued every day. Because I need it every day. I can't save myself. I've tried. It doesn't end well. I can't right the ship. I can't pull myself out of the deep end of the pool. I need a rescuer.

I think this might be why Pharisees, fundamentalists, and the legalists within us all resist grace. To receive grace, we need to come out of hiding, acknowledge our weakness, confess our limitations, and receive help. Legalism believes the lie that I can do it on my own. I can keep the rules. I just need to work a little harder. We cling to the old way of the law, working to measure up. Jesus overturns the old to bring a new way, a grace-and-truth way.

Jesus entered the temple courts and drove out all who were buying and selling there. He overturned the tables of the money changers and the benches of those selling doves. "'It is written,' he said to them, 'My house will be called a house of prayer,' but you are making it 'a den of robbers.'"[7]

I used to think these verses were about Jesus being upset about selling things in church. And maybe they are. But I see more here. I see Jesus overturning a religious and commercial system that said *you* must make the offering for your sin. The people supporting the system of sacrifice, the money changers and buyers and sellers, were robbing the people of grace. Jesus, God himself, full of grace and truth, stood there among them—and they kept buying and selling stuff to sacrifice. I do the same thing still. A lot.

I face the choice each day: Receive grace, or measure. One day, as I was praying and feeling very lost and "less than," God opened up this scene with Jesus in the temple. And Jesus was mad. As he turned the tables over, I saw a table covered with beakers (think back to your high school chemistry lab) all filled to different levels with liquids of different colors. In his anger, Jesus flipped the table. The beakers smashed to the ground, glass flew, and the colored liquid flowed everywhere. Then the scene flipped, and I saw all the beakers, empty, piled up under the cross. As the life of Jesus flowed down from the cross, the beakers filled to overflowing.

And the Lord spoke: "I do not measure you the way you do. This is how I measure you."

I was living my life measuring me by my standards—which by the way, I thought were God's standards. Hear the lie of not enough? I was always measuring. Is it good enough? Is the sacrifice acceptable? The quiet times haven't been long enough. I've watched too much TV, eaten too much sugar, spent too much on Amazon. All the reasons I didn't measure up. But God doesn't look at any of it. He looks at Jesus. And the beakers are full. In Him, I am enough. And this is grace. This is a place I can breathe.

Grace invites us to return to blessing, to the place of living out in the open—connected with God, with ourselves, with one another. To return to the garden before the snake, before the apple, before shame. Grace rescues us from the impossible task of proving and fixing and restoring ourselves. We simply can't do it. All these efforts end only in perfectionism that suffocates the spirit and kills the soul. Father Richard Rohr writes:

> Most of us were not raised to understand that we are participating in something that is already happening. Rather, we were given tasks to accomplish individually and completely. This placed the entire burden on the single isolated person. That's not participation. That's perfectionism—thinking I have to do it all or that I can do it all (the American myth). I'm convinced that's why we have so much of what we call negative self-image in the West—because of this impossible spiritual burden put on the separate individual. The Good News is that it's not about being correct. It's about being connected. When the Spirit within you connects with God's Spirit given from without, you are finally home.[8]

NECESSARY WEAKNESS

Jacob, son of Isaac and grandson of Abraham, the one who would become Israel, had deceived his father and stolen his brother Esau's birthright.[9] Now Jacob was on the run because Esau was coming after him to kill him. Jacob's very name meant "to grasp the heal," and he'd been grasping all his life for blessing that was not legally his. Alone in the desert, he laid his head on a stone and fell asleep. As he dreamed he saw a ladder with angels ascending and descending from Earth to heaven. And God spoke.

> I am the LORD, THE GOD OF YOUR FATHER ABRAHAM AND THE GOD OF ISAAC. I WILL GIVE YOU AND YOUR DESCENDANTS THE LAND ON WHICH YOU ARE LYING. Your descendants will be like the dust of the earth, and you will spread out to the west and to the east, to the north and to the south. All peoples on earth will be blessed through you and your offspring. I am with you and will watch over you wherever you go, and I will bring you back to this land. I will not leave you until I have done what I have promised you.

In the morning Jacob awakened from his sleep and said, "Surely the LORD is in this place, and I was not aware of it. . . . How awesome is this place! This is none other than the house of God; this is the gate of heaven."

The promise of a land and people and blessing—all came unmerited to this grasper. All came as grace. Author Kathleen Norris writes:

> God does not punish Jacob as he lies sleeping because he can see in him Israel, the foundation of a people. God loves to look at us, and loves it when we will look back at him. Even when we try to run away from our troubles, as Jacob did, God will find us, and bless us, even when we feel most alone, unsure if we'll survive the night. God will find a way to let us know that he is with us in this place, wherever we are, however far we think we've run. And maybe that's one reason we worship—to respond to grace.[10]

God comes to meet us in the lonely, desperate, grasping, deceiving places of our lives. Not after it's all set right, cleaned

up, and packaged with a bow. Grace runs right into the middle of
the mess to fill and empower the promise. The apostle Paul, writer
of much of the New Testament, knew this to be true. In prison, he
asked the Lord three times to restore him. God's answer to this
prayer was grace.

> Three times I pleaded with the Lord to take it away from
> me. But he said to me, "My grace is sufficient for you, for my
> power is made perfect in weakness." Therefore I will boast
> all the more gladly about my weaknesses, so that Christ's
> power may rest on me. That is why, for Christ's sake, I delight
> in weaknesses, in insults, in hardships, in persecutions, in
> difficulties. For when I am weak, then I am strong.[11]

Weakness is gift because the weak, empty places in me make
space for grace—for God (IN) me to be strength. For grace to fill the
lack. In my weakness, he is strong. Right in the middle of it. I love
this, but I don't like it very much at all. It requires vulnerability. An
experience of grace requires weakness, a certain desperation, an
acknowledgment of my need, a cry to be rescued. Brené Brown says
(and I think she's so right) that we live wholeheartedly only as we
learn to receive our imperfections as gifts:

> It's about the willingness to be imperfect, to be vulner-
> able. It's about the courage to wake up in the morning and
> acknowledge that no matter what gets done and what doesn't
> get done, that I'm enough, and that I'm worthy of love, belong-
> ing, and joy. Those are irreducible needs for humans.
>   The opposite of it is scarcity: "I'm not enough." What
> I produce, what I create, dictates who I am and dictates
> my worth. Wholeheartedness is different than that. It's,
> "I am enough."[12]

TURNING

I'm a lot like Jacob. Maybe you are, too. I'm grasping, striving, working, trying to make the blessing happen in my own power. Forgetting
that grace has already been given. I'm missing the mark all the time.
Grace says all I need to do is acknowledge the missing and return.

Sometimes words used in the Bible and in church have come to
carry shame for some of us. Words like "repent" and "confess" can feel
heavy and condemning. But both are invitations to grace. In Greek, the
word "repentance" means "to change one's mind" or "to choose to think
differently." The word "confess" means to "agree, admit, acknowledge."
This same idea exists in the Hebrew word *tshuva*, usually translated as
repentance. The Hebrew verb literally means "a turning." In *tshuva*,
one returns to the right path, the path that has always been present.

Do you feel lost? Unworthy? Unwanted? Not enough? Too much?
Grace invites you out of hiding into the open to simply acknowledge it
and return. Admit your reality, the dark and light together, and invite
Jesus to be present in all of it. Ask him to show you what's really true—
how he sees you and your story. In this vulnerable place, connection is
restored as grace and truth come together. From here, you can return
to what's been true about you, about your life the whole time.

Grace empowers us to choose, to move toward the truth about
us and the truth about God. Grace returns us to love. This path has
always been present. You have always been fully loved. God has always
been fully good. You just wandered off for a bit. And now you are
invited home. French author Jacques Philippe echoes the invitation:

> What often blocks the action of God's grace in our lives
> is less our sins or failings, than it is our failure to accept
> our own weakness—all those rejections, conscious or not, of
> what we really are or of our real situation. To "set grace free"
> in our lives, and paving the way for deep and spectacular

changes, it sometimes would be enough to say simply "yes"—
a "yes" inspired by trust in God to aspects of our lives we've
been rejecting. We refuse to admit that we have this defect,
that weak point, were marked by this event, fell into that
sin. And so we block the Holy Spirit's action, since he can
only affect our reality to the extent we accept it ourselves.[13]

How is God inviting you today to turn, to acknowledge the
things in the way of grace? Socrates said, "The unexamined life is
not worth living." St. Ignatius of Loyola agreed, but probably for different reasons. Ignatian spirituality offers us the Prayer of Examen.
Richard Foster describes the Prayer of Examen in this way: "It has
two basic aspects, like two sides of a door. The first is an examen of
consciousness through which we discover how God has been present
to us throughout the day and how we have responded to his loving
presence. The second aspect is an examen of conscience in which we
uncover those areas that need cleansing, purifying, and healing."
Foster goes on to describe these two aspects of examen for us:

> In the examen of consciousness we prayerfully reflect
> on the thoughts, feelings and actions of our days to see how
> God has been at work among us and how we responded.... In
> the examen of conscience we are inviting the Lord to search
> our hearts to the depths. Far from being dreadful, this is a
> scrutiny of love.... Without apology and without defense we
> ask to see what is truly in us. It is for our own sake that we
> ask these things. It is for our good, for our healing, for our
> happiness.[14]

We are incapable of knowing what is truly within us apart from
the searching love of Holy Spirit. When we allow the Spirit to search
us and to expose where we are off the path, he invites us again to

acknowledge, to turn. It is this practice of examen and repentance that helps us live rooted and remaining in love.

GRACE AND TRUTH

In some places, if you talk too much about grace, someone is likely to remind you about truth. "Don't forget, you need the truth too." As if truth and grace were opposites. Or needed to be balanced on a scale. In Jesus, we find grace and truth embodied. They must be held together, because when they meet, something extraordinary happens.

"Mercy and truth are met together; righteousness and peace have kissed each other."[15]

When we add conditions to grace, we lose the beauty and intimacy of this kiss. We make grace small and weak. We make Jesus small and weak. We say, in essence, that God's love isn't strong enough to hold us. That his promises aren't strong enough to be true. I tend to think that when God says, "I will never leave you or forsake you," he means it.

I choose grace as grace chooses me. And this grace holds me until the end. Grace rooted and grounded in the love of God. It is grace, God's kindness, that draws me to turn, and turn again, to him, to life. It is grace, God's power, that enables me to stay on the path. It is grace. All grace. I can't add to it. I can only run to it. Because who could deny a love that strong?

> You are so weak. Give up to grace.
> The ocean takes care of each wave till it gets to shore.
> You need more help than you know.
>
> —RUMI[16]

DEEPER (IN)

Examen is an invitation to live more conscious of when I am living (IN) God and when I am not. Every day is full of both for me. The moments I choose to love and serve my daughter with gratitude for her life and patience for her growth—and the moments when I snap at her for leaving the dirty laundry on the floor right next to the hamper (I mean really, right next to it). Taking time, silent moments each day, to reflect on these in and out moments in the light of God's love allows me to practice both gratitude and repentance. And in both, I live again more fully (IN) God.

Prayer of Examen

What does the Prayer of Examen look like? One version of the Daily Examen from St. Ignatius looks like this:

1. Become aware of God's presence.
2. Review the day with gratitude.
3. Pay attention to your emotions.
4. Choose one feature of the day and pray from it.
5. Look toward tomorrow.

You can learn more at: http://www.ignatianspirituality.com/ignatian-prayer/the-examen.

Set aside ten minutes at the end of your day to pray through the five prompts above. What comes to mind as you prayerfully reflect on the day? What are you grateful for? What was hard? How was God present?

Grace upon Grace

As you read this chapter, did any areas of shame or weakness come to mind? Places where you need grace? As you hold this area before the Lord, read these words from John 1:14, 16–18 slowly. What images come to mind as you read? What new grace does God want to give you today? How does he want to meet you in your weakness?

> The Word became flesh and made his dwelling among us. We have seen his glory, the glory of the one and only Son, who came from the Father, full of grace and truth. . . .
>
> Out of his fullness we have all received grace in place of grace already given. For the law was given through Moses; grace and truth came through Jesus Christ. No one has ever seen God, but the one and only Son, who is himself God and is in closest relationship with the Father, has made him known.

A Prayer from Thomas Merton

My Lord God,

I have no idea where I am going.

I do not see the road ahead of me.

I cannot know for certain where it will end.

nor do I really know myself,

and the fact that I think I am following your will

does not mean that I am actually doing so.

But I believe that the desire to please you

does in fact please you.

And I hope I have that desire in all that I am doing.

I hope that I will never do anything apart from that desire.

And I know that if I do this you will lead me by the right road,

though I may know nothing about it.

Therefore will I trust you always though

I may seem to be lost and in the shadow of death.

I will not fear, for you are ever with me,

and you will never leave me to face my perils alone.[17]

PART THREE

◆

LOVING YOURSELF AND OTHERS

CHAPTER 9

◆

(IN) Truth

A self is not something static, tied up in a pretty parcel
and handed to the child, finished and complete.
A self is always becoming.
—MADELEINE L'ENGLE[1]

I FELT STUCK. I'd known for years that I was called to write, and I wasn't doing it. And I had lots of excuses for not doing it. Life is busy, after all.

Finally, at our strategic planning day in 2017, my Roots&Branches board (I have the best board) called me out. They told me I needed to write. Now. And they made it part of my job—one of my goals. They set other priorities aside and said, write. I felt grateful. And terrified. Now I had no more excuses. I had to face the blank page.

I've done other writing in my life—articles, curricula, marketing materials. But never a book. A book felt too big. A book requires a lot of words and thoughts. And as I stared at the blank page, I realized the lie of "not enough" was right there with me. I didn't believe I had enough to say, enough words to write. I didn't believe I was worthy of being published. It was "not enough" all over the place.

This lie of not enough had rooted deeply in my soul as a child. And the lie led to legalism, as all lies do. I must do something (or not do something) to be OK. I must excel, be the best, be the brightest. It was a lot of pressure on an extremely shy, lonely little girl. But I was smart and good at school, so I chased A's and fell into a trap. I vested my

141

identity in my performance, with the unattainable goal of perfection. And the lie repeated over and over: You are not enough.

My greatest fear, as I journeyed into healing in my twenties, was that, at the very center of me was nothing. I was only the sum of what I'd built up around me. All the successes were my hiding places. Successes that were ultimately defenses, protecting me, or so I thought, from being seen and found lacking. I was sure if people could see me, the real me, they would see I was nothing at all. In her book *Captivating*, Stacy Eldredge described me as if she knew me:

> We hide our truest selves and offer only what we believe is wanted, what is safe. We act in self-protective ways and refuse to offer what we truly see, believe, and know. We will not risk rejection or looking like a fool. We have spoken in the past and been met with blank stares and mocking guffaws. We will not do it again. We hide because we are afraid.[2]

The shame of not enough kept me hidden. Performing. Perfecting. Creating something I thought others would find acceptable. And I lost me—or perhaps I just hadn't found me. Or maybe I was just too afraid to be me. Because being me was not enough.

So here I was in my fifties, having received so much healing and truth over years, feeling stuck. I was trying to write this book, and it felt like trying to push a boulder up a mountain. Now I don't think writing always comes with flow. Writing is sometimes just the work of putting words on the page. But I knew something was in the way. "Not enough" was in the way.

So I went away. I retreated to Fall Creek Abbey in Indianapolis for a few days. Dave and Beth Booram run this magical little retreat right in their home. It is thick with peace, beauty, creativity, and the fragrance of rest. I asked Beth, a spiritual director, for some time together. I described how I was feeling, pushing the boulder that was my book up the mountain. We sat together in silence for a while, allowing me space to listen. She asked some questions. Where is God in this process? What is he inviting you to? Really good questions.

As we talked and listened together, she offered a picture: "You feel like you're going uphill, pushing to make this happen, all by yourself. I see you stepping onto a bridge. And writing this book with Jesus is how you get to the other side. It's the writing with Jesus that takes you where you need to go. You can't get there any other way."

In that moment, with that picture, light broke in. I realized the lie of "not enough" was leaving me all alone, working, striving to make this book happen myself. Yes, I'd asked God for help writing. Like he was somewhere out there rather than right here, in me. I wasn't writing in connection, with the living Word who is always speaking. In him, there is always enough.

So I sat with Jesus, asking him to remind me of what was true. To root me again in love. To help me bring my writing into a more connected place with him. In him. I released every thought that writing this book was about getting published. I released the fear of the book and me not being enough. And I embraced the journey knowing that this work of writing, right now in this moment with Jesus, this is the gift. And in this moment, there is enough. I am enough.

WHAT'S IN A NAME?

"You are my beloved son." These are identity words, the Father naming Jesus. Beloved son. Apparently, Jesus needed to hear this. And we need to hear this, too, deep in our souls where it can stick. We believe a lot of things about ourselves that aren't true. Lies come at us from the shadows, from our culture, from marketers, sometimes sadly from family and friends. God names us to remind us who we really are.

The disciples had been with Jesus for a while now. They were his closest companions, living together day and night on a three-year road trip. They'd seen it all, heard it all. The miracles, the messages. One day, as they were together, Jesus asks them a clarifying question.[3] "Who do you say I am?" Simon Peter is the first to answer. "You are the Messiah, the son of the living God."

With this declaration, Simon Peter becomes Peter. "Blessed are you, Simon son of Jonah, for this was not revealed to you by flesh and blood, but by my Father in heaven. And I tell you that you are Peter, and on this rock I will build my church, and the gates of Hades will not overcome it."

Jesus is not giving Peter an assignment. Jesus is telling him who he really is. Who he has been all along. Even before he met Jesus, when he was Simon Peter the fisherman, he was Peter. The Rock. And from this identity comes Peter's destiny. But not all of Peter knows this yet. There's some false that must be healed and restored as Peter learns to live in the true. Because this is the same Peter who will do some impetuous things. Some terrible things. He'll cut off a guard's ear when they come to arrest Jesus. He'll deny his friend three times on the night before he is crucified. And shame will send him back to living as Simon Peter, the fisherman.

Post-resurrection, Jesus comes to make breakfast for his friends on the beach.[4] Simon Peter and two other disciples have been fishing all night and don't have much to show for it. Jesus calls out to them, telling them to throw the net to the other side of the boat. As they pull in a miraculous, massive haul of fish, Simon recognizes Jesus. He jumps in the water and swims to shore. (Did I mention he's a bit impetuous?) After a breakfast of fish and bread, Jesus begins the work of restoration.

> When they had finished eating, Jesus said to Simon Peter, "Simon son of John, do you love me more than these?"
>
> "Yes, Lord," he said, "you know that I love you."
>
> Jesus said, "Feed my lambs."
>
> Again Jesus said, "Simon son of John, do you love me?"
>
> He answered, "Yes, Lord, you know that I love you."

Jesus said, "Take care of my sheep."

The third time he said to him, "Simon son of John, do you love me?"

Peter was hurt because Jesus asked him the third time, "Do you love me?"

He said, "Lord, you know all things; you know that I love you."

Jesus said, "Feed my sheep. Very truly I tell you, when you were younger you dressed yourself and went where you wanted; but when you are old you will stretch out your hands, and someone else will dress you and lead you where you do not want to go." Jesus said this to indicate the kind of death by which Peter would glorify God. Then he said to him, "Follow me!"

Jesus speaks to Simon the fisherman, inviting him to step back into his true Peter self. I think Peter is hurt when Jesus asks the question a third time, because it echoes the three times Peter denied knowing Jesus. There on the beach, Jesus takes Peter back to that place of denial and shame to restore him, to reinstate him, and to remind him who he really is. The Rock. The one who *will* follow Jesus to his own death. Ultimately, Peter would be crucified upside down because he did not want the honor of dying in the same way Jesus died. In the end, Peter lives and dies in the truth of who he is and who he has become, the Rock.

In many ways, the journey is the same for all of us. We go about our daily business—fishing, parenting, working, playing, buying, selling. As we encounter Jesus, we find we are more. He names us "beloved," reminding us of what is already true. And in this identity we find our destiny, the invitation to the adventure of our lives. Then along the way, we forget. We go back to finding our identity in fishing, parenting, working, playing, buying, selling. And we need to be reminded and healed and restored. Again and again he comes to remind us, you are more than what you see, what you've experienced, what you do. You are beloved. You are friend. You are son and daughter. We are one. You in me. Me in you. Living rooted and grounded in this truth, we like Peter live more and more as the people we are and the people we are becoming.

WHAT'S TRUE

When we get quiet, we know it. We feel it. We were made for more than what we're experiencing in our lives today. For life in the garden. Connected. No hiding. No shame. And we still long for this, for the perfect. For life before it went off the rails. We feel the gap—the distance between the ideal we long for and the real of the life we experience. We long for perfection, fullness, the joy of union, connected relationship with God, with our true selves and with others. And in the longing, the realizing we're missing the mark, shame and everything false finds a dwelling place. We spend our lives working to fill the gap, to present to the world something closer to the ideal we long for.

Many of us find a place to hide in perfectionism, working ourselves to exhaustion trying to present a Martha-Stewart-Pinterest-worthy-Instagrammable life to the world. Did I mention it's exhausting? All the hiding and perfecting and presenting, living in all the false, is a life-sucking existence. But we choose it because it feels safer than the honest truth: that we are weak, we are bent, and we don't really know who we are.

"Be perfect, therefore, as your heavenly Father is perfect."[5]

Hold on a minute. These are words of Jesus—the one who invites us to live in the real, in the now, coming out of hiding into the open. What does he mean when he says we are to be perfect?

The word for "perfect" here is *teleios*. It means essentially to be complete, fully mature. To become more completely, more fully ourselves. In the words of Kathleen Norris, *teleios* perfection "demands that we become fully ourselves as God would have us: mature, ripe, full, ready for what befalls you, for whatever is to come."[6]

As God lives in us, as we live in him, we are becoming *teleios*. He is not a hard father meanly setting an unmeetable standard. He is a good father inviting us to live rooted and remaining, acknowledging the false and more fully becoming the true. In loving relationship with him, we are becoming perfect because the perfect, the holy, the whole, already dwells within.

> God is love. Whoever lives in love lives in God, and God in them. This is how love is made complete among us so that we will have confidence on the day of judgment: In this world we are like Jesus. There is no fear in love. But perfect love drives out fear, because fear has to do with punishment. The one who fears is not made perfect in love.
>
> We love because he first loved us.[7]

Here's the word *teleios* again. We are being made perfect in love. No fear. No hiding. In love, we live in God and God lives in us. This is how love is made complete in us and we are made complete in love. In the world we look and live more and more like Jesus. And it all begins with knowing his love for us. I don't muster up the love. I don't work hard to be worthy of the love. I receive the free gift. This kind of transformation, empowered by grace, requires trust, yielding, and remaining as God works in us both to will and to do. To take off the old and false. To put on the new.

Your true self is the real, original, authentic you. This is the you known and loved by God before anything came into being. It's the you that you are and that you're becoming, the perfect you, uniquely fashioned and fitted to bring Jesus into the world. Your identity, the true you, is established (IN) Christ. Theologian and author Eugene Peterson writes:

> My identity does not begin when I begin to understand
> myself. There is something previous to what I think about

myself, and it is what God thinks of me. That means that
everything I think and feel is by nature a response, and the
one to whom I respond is God. I never speak the first word.
I never make the first move.[8]

Your false self, the self you put on or take on, the mask you wear,
doesn't yet know this love. Outside of love, the false looks like offense,
pride, judgment, ego, separation, and disconnection. Here in the false,
we live divided from God, from ourselves and from others. Truth teaches
us another way to live.

That, however, is not the way of life you learned when
you heard about Christ and were taught in him in accor-
dance with the truth that is in Jesus. You were taught, with
regard to your former way of life, to put off your old self,
which is being corrupted by its deceitful desires; to be
made new in the attitude of your minds; and to put on the
new self, created to be like God in true righteousness and
holiness.[9]

As we see the true and false in our lives, we are invited to make
an exchange, the old for the new. We are invited to an unveiling.

THE UNVEILING

Mary and Martha sent a message to their friend, Jesus.[10] "Lord, the
one you love is sick." Their brother Lazarus was sick, and they knew
Jesus could help. If Jesus was there, their brother would be healed.
When Jesus got this news, he did not exhibit normal good friend kind
of behavior. He waited two days to leave; he waited for Lazarus to die.
Ready at last to make the trip, Jesus tells his companions, "Our friend
Lazarus has fallen asleep; but I am going there to wake him up." When
they suggested that sleep might be good for a sick person, Jesus told

them plainly, "Lazarus is dead, and for your sake I am glad I was not there, so that you may believe."

When Jesus arrives on the scene, Lazarus has been in the tomb three days, and the community is in mourning. Jesus, moved by compassion, weeps with them. Then it gets really interesting.

> Jesus, once more deeply moved, came to the tomb. It was a cave with a stone laid across the entrance. "Take away the stone," he said.
>
> "But, Lord," said Martha, the sister of the dead man, "by this time there is a bad odor, for he has been there four days."
>
> Then Jesus said, "Did I not tell you that if you believe, you will see the glory of God?"
>
> So they took away the stone. Then Jesus looked up and said, "Father, I thank you that you have heard me. I knew that you always hear me, but I said this for the benefit of the people standing here, that they may believe that you sent me."
>
> When he had said this, Jesus called in a loud voice, "Lazarus, come out!" The dead man came out, his hands and feet wrapped with strips of linen, and a cloth around his face. Jesus said to them, "Take off the grave clothes and let him go."

Jesus comes to awaken Lazarus, and Lazarus emerges, stepping from death to life. Resurrection. It's a foretelling of what is about to happen to Jesus, emerging from the tomb. Life coming from death. It's also a beautiful picture of all of us. Jesus comes to awaken us from our slumber, to call our true selves from death to life, and to begin to remove our grave clothes, all the layers of false that smell of death. The old is removed to reveal the true, the eternal.

I've had the honor of sitting now with hundreds in prayer, hearing their stories and holding sacred space, inviting Jesus to be present in their pain. Shame, pain, disappointment, and loss have shrouded them. They have lived hidden beneath layers of self-protection, addiction, anger, self-harm, and more. These layers, our grave clothes, have lots of names.

Yet beneath all these layers, as I've listened and been present with people in their pain, I've seen again and again the beauty and glory of the human spirit. This beauty has been hidden beneath layers of false self, sometimes nearly smothered under its weight. Hope and joy snuffed out. As we listen and pray, God comes to awaken hearts and remove the layers. He reveals the things that block, hinder, and bind the real; and replaces the false with true. The old self gives way to the new self, created to be like God.

Separated from God and from our true selves, we are Lazarus in the tomb, mummies, shadows of ourselves. Our layers of accomplishments, control, pleasures, pride, and power give us shape but no substance. The layers must be removed. We must be, as the apostle Paul says, unveiled.

> And we all, who with unveiled faces contemplate the Lord's glory, are being transformed into his image with ever-increasing glory, which comes from the Lord, who is the Spirit.[11]

Jesus comes by Spirit into the center of our experience to reveal us as ourselves. He comes, kind and firm, to remove the veils, and to show us where we've missed the mark. Where disappointment and trauma and grief and fear have done their work to bend us into something other than ourselves. He comes in love to restore what's been in us all along, and to allow what's deepest in us to emerge. Our journey with him is one of becoming who we already are, created with purpose and beauty, carrying the glory of God. "It is a beautiful paradox," writes Stasi Eldredge, "that the more God's we become, the more ourselves we become—the 'self' he had in mind when he thought of you before the creation of the world."[12]

ROOTED IN TRUTH

Remember the identity words spoken by the Father over Jesus at his baptism? "You are my beloved son." This blessing, this favor, is given to us as well. And we need it. We need to hear it over and over again. Because the world around us and everything false is telling us something different. All the time.

We are beloved sons, beloved daughters, beloved ones. This is our identity. If "beloved" feels like a hard word to access, think instead of deeply loved, without condition. Held in love as son or daughter. The son or daughter you would never reject and always pursue. The child you gaze on with deep wonder and delight. This, beloved, is you.

"Self-rejection," writes Henri Nouwen, "is the greatest enemy of the spiritual life because it contradicts the sacred voice that calls us the 'Beloved.' Being the Beloved constitutes the core truth of our existence."[13] Our souls need to hear these words of blessing and belovedness. The words must go deeper than our thoughts. This knowing that we are known, seen, chosen, created in love must penetrate our hearts so that it can reside in us and begin to change us. This is the deep knowing we can live from, the place we can trust God to come and begin the healing work of removing the layers of false.

There's a little news here that might disappoint: This process of becoming our true selves, living in our belovedness, it takes time. A lifetime, in fact. It doesn't happen like magic, with the wave of a wand or a prayer of deliverance. It happens as we listen and live connected with the One who knows what's true about us better than we do. It happens as we live connected with others who will bless this truth in us. And it happens as we begin to hold our lives up to God, asking him to search us, to reveal the false and bring the true. As we listen to God within, hearing what is true, beginning to live in what is true, the layers of false are slowly peeled away revealing more true. Revealing more you.

TRUE PRAYER

King David lived something of a salty life. Murder. Stealing another man's wife. That kind of thing. Salty. And yet he was known as a man after God's own heart. He was a man who knew how to enter God's presence, through song, through ritual (kind of like sacraments), through dance, through prayer. King David saw and understood, at least in part, the wonder of who he was, knit together with intention, always seen, always known. God had formed his inmost self—his mind and emotions, soul and spirit—all that was most truly David. And all this was wonderful.

> For you created my inmost being;
> you knit me together in my mother's womb.
> I praise you because I am fearfully and wonderfully made;
> your works are wonderful,
> I know that full well.
> My frame was not hidden from you
> when I was made in the secret place,
> when I was woven together in the depths of the earth.
> Your eyes saw my unformed body;
> all the days ordained for me were written in your book
> before one of them came to be.

From this place of knowing, the place of trust, David was able to pray a bold prayer. He asked God to search his life.

> Search me, God, and know my heart;
> test me and know my anxious thoughts.

See if there is any offensive way in me,
and lead me in the way everlasting.[14]

The word "offensive" here can have two meanings: It can refer to pain and sorrow; it can also refer to the worship of an idol, following the false. Since the following of the false brings pain and sorrow, I wonder if here the two might be connected. "God, show me any way I'm living by something false. Show me the source of the pain I'm experiencing. What am I anxious about? Why is there no peace in this place?" David asks God because he can't see it for himself. We usually can't see it for ourselves either. We know something is wrong. We feel the pain, the stress, the anxiety. We see behaviors and reactions that are destructive, but we don't always know the source. We need Spirit to speak, to test, to illuminate what's within.

In my own life, as I've been writing this book, I've been aware of some anxiety. The thought that kept coming was: You don't have enough to say. Finally, I stopped to ask and listen. "God, what's this anxiety about? Where's it coming from?"

A scene from grade school came to mind immediately, something I hadn't thought about for years. In the middle of third grade, we'd moved from Cincinnati to Lexington. The first day at this new school, I realized they'd already learned their multiplication tables. I hadn't even begun. I was the new girl, without a friend in the room, already very behind. And for a little girl who found her identity in her grades (yes, even that early), behind was not OK. Behind meant I didn't have enough to keep up. It meant I wasn't enough. This sense of being behind, of not enough, had attached not only to math but to all my subjects. It had attached to my writing.

As I saw this scene, I invited Jesus to show me where he was, what he was doing—to show the little girl who felt behind what was true. I saw him there with me, in the classroom, smiling big and paying no attention to the teacher. He was focused only on me. I was focused only on him. Jesus began to tell me what was true. I don't remember the exact words. I just remember knowing that a place that felt painful and produced anxiety for that little girl now felt safe. I felt connected with Jesus and the truth he brought. And in that place, I knew I was loved. I was enough.

Jesus met Peter on a beach. He met me in third grade. In just a few minutes, something that had been blocking my writing was removed. Another layer of not enough was lifted off, and I could breathe freer air. The thought still comes sometimes: You don't have enough to say. But I have a place of truth to stand now, and I can stare it down. I can hold up the truth I've been given and live from a new place of grace. Maybe this is why the apostle Paul ends so many of his letters with this same blessing: "Grace and peace to you." We need this blessing again and again. Grace. Peace. Remember, you are beloved.

DEEPER (IN)

Listening Prayer: Psalm 139

"For me to be a saint means to be myself. Therefore the problem of sanctity and salvation is in fact the problem of finding out who I am and of discovering my true self."

—Thomas Merton[15]

Set aside fifteen minutes or so and find a quiet space. In a Bible or online, go to Psalm 139. Take a few deep breaths and bless God's presence with you and in you. Read the psalm slowly at least two times, pausing to let the words speak to you. Feeling bold? Now pray David's prayer.[16]

Search me, God, and know my heart;
　　test me and know my anxious thoughts.
See if there is any offensive way in me,
　　and lead me in the way everlasting.

1. *Rest.* Take a few deep breaths. Relax. Invite God's presence.

2. *Receive.* Ask Holy Spirit to reveal any worry or anxiety. Listen. Is there an anxious or worried place inside? What comes to mind? A thought? A picture? A memory? An emotion? Invite Jesus to show you what you need to know about what you're sensing. How does he want to be present in it with you? Ask him if there's anything you're believing that isn't true; then ask him what really is true in this situation.

3. *Respond.* How would you like to respond to what he's showing you? Is there something to release? Something to receive? Respond to the invitation you sense from God. Ask him to replace the lie with the truth.

4. *Remain.* Now simply rest in God's presence.

CHAPTER 10

◆

(IN) Light

There is no greater agony than
bearing an untold story inside you.
—MAYA ANGELOU[1]

I WAS SOBBING. On the elliptical. At the Y.

Oprah was on all the televisions lined up in front of our row of workout machines. She was bringing Christmas to hundreds of children orphaned by AIDS in Africa in a way only Oprah could. And I was sobbing. I didn't care if others were watching. I was a part of what was happening in front of me, and I knew I couldn't stop crying no matter how hard I tried. Something deep within me was connecting with the story of these children.

It was 2004, nine years after I'd stepped away from the ministry to people with HIV/AIDS in Cincinnati. I'd handed over the leadership to a friend because I'd just gotten married and become a stepmom. We needed to blend a family. Working full-time and nurturing this new family would require all the energy and focus I had to give. I grieved the loss of this ministry deeply. And as I grieved, I heard the whisper in my soul, "I will bring this back around in your life. This is not the end." I had no idea what that meant; but I held it, pondered it, and wondered.

There in the Y, I felt as if an invisible hand was pointing at the television. And I heard the whisper. "This. Here. This is for you."

My response to the invitation was a strong and immediate "No way." AIDS in Africa? This is too big. Too much. Thank you. But no. As the show ended, I dried my eyes, stepped off the elliptical, and walked away.

But God was unrelenting in his invitation. I could not get those children out of my mind. A few weeks later, I was talking with my friend Shannon, who is a U2 superfan. She travels all over the world to be part of U2 concert events. Yes, she is that cool. We were talking about Bono's work with AIDS in Africa. As my eyes began to water, words I'd never actually thought came out of my mouth. "I hope I get to go." I was stunned. Apparently, the deepest part of me was responding to the invitation. As I left her home, I stopped on the sidewalk, and breathed a prayer. "OK. If you want to do this, I say yes. I have no idea how this would ever happen. But if you make the way, I'm in."

A week later, I was participating in a class at church. As we were talking about how we can discover and live in our gifts and passions, a woman started sharing about her husband's passion for HIV/AIDS care and prevention in Africa. A chill ran all the way up my back. After class I made a beeline to this woman to ask questions. What was her husband doing? As I spoke with her, and as I spoke later with her husband, I learned he was part of a team starting a ministry. They were making a trip to South Africa in six weeks. Did I want to come along?

I had the same response I'd had in the Y. That's too big. Too soon. Too expensive. Do people just decide to go to Africa in six weeks? I didn't even have a passport. No. I wasn't going.

When I told my husband about the invitation and my response, he strongly and lovingly pushed back. "Susan, I think God can get you to Africa in six weeks. We can expedite a passport. I think you should do this."

And with that, my no went to yes. Six weeks later I was on a plane headed to Johannesburg. We spent ten days in and around Soweto, meeting with people, finding out about needs, building a team that would come together to do youth development work, all with the aim of preventing the spread of HIV/AIDS.

Marcia Ball and Jennie Cerullo were part of that team. I liked them immediately. Founders and directors of Kerus Global Education, they had traveled the world working with children and youth in HIV/AIDS prevention. Now they were focusing in South Africa with plans to open an orphan care center. Their ministry was growing through partnerships, and they needed someone to help with writing and curriculum development. As our friendship formed over those first days, we began to wonder together if I might be the person to help them. I'd worked in curriculum development and writing for more than twenty years. This was my kind of gig. God's invitation kept getting bigger.

I came home promising to pray and to talk with my husband about the opportunity. I lived in Cincinnati. Jennie and Marcia lived in Harrisburg, Virginia. And the children lived in South Africa. I needed or at least wanted confirmation that this was what God had in mind.

I attended a silent retreat with the intention of listening and discerning. In the silence, I walked a prayer labyrinth, asking, listening. Stepping into the center of the labyrinth, I looked down to see a pen on the ground. Right smack in the center of the labyrinth. I picked up the pen, and my mouth dropped open in a silent gasp. The pen said "South Africa." (You can't make this stuff up, people.)

Other women shared the labyrinth with me, some walking ahead, some walking behind, all in silence. I asked the group later; no one else on the labyrinth had seen that pen. No one had dropped that pen. It seems the pen was there just for me, a writing implement with the words "South Africa" on it. Yes, I know it sounds a little crazy. And I know God isn't always this obvious and direct. In fact, my life rarely works this way. But apparently this time, God decided I needed a push.

I joined the Kerus team for some of the best and most exciting work of my life. The story that started with AIDS ministry in Cincinnati hadn't ended at all. It was just the beginning. The first stanza, the first chapter, the first few brushstrokes of the larger creative work of my life. God was speaking a story into existence that crossed continents.

LET THERE BE LIGHT

God spoke. And light and life came forth through Jesus. The Word made flesh, present and giving life from the start. This is the story we are given by the apostle John of the beginning. Living things born from spoken word. Living things are still being born and reborn as God speaks. You are being born, becoming more you, as he speaks words of light and life in you. Our lives are spoken word. Poetry, rap, story with rhythm and beauty meant to be owned, lived fully in the light, and shared out loud.

And I need the light. Because I find I don't know my own story very well. The true and false that are me blend together in a way that can make the one indistinguishable from the other. I have no idea why I do what I do much of the time. The things I want to do, I don't do. The things I don't want to do, I do. It's a timeless dilemma. For most every effect in my life, there is a cause. There is a root. And I need the light to find it.

The parts of our story we keep hidden, the parts that feel too dangerous or painful or shameful to put on the table in broad daylight, these parts hold power. In these parts of our story, we find the roots that keep us tethered to the pain and shame. And these roots keep us living from the false, the lies we learned there about ourselves and about God.

Dr. Brené Brown says, "Owning our stories and loving ourselves through that process is the bravest thing we will ever do."[2] This is courageous work. The shame and guilt and pain are loud. We are afraid they will overwhelm us. They tell us that the less pleasant and very painful parts of our stories are unlovable. That we are unlovable. Kept hidden, these parts hold sway. Out in the open, in the light, they start to lose their power.

Owning my story means taking a full-on, out-in-the-light look at all of it. Yes, all of it. With brutal honesty. A Bono quote seems appropriate here (you know, because of the South Africa thing and all):

> We don't have to please God in any other way than to be brutally honest. That is the root. Not just to a relationship with God, but it's the root to a great song. That's the only place you can find a great song. The only place you can find any work of art, of merit.[3]

The creative, coming-into-being, true self work of our life requires we live our life progressively, more and more in the light. Out in the open. It means honestly owning the highs and lows, the best and worst together. Holding it all before God, watching for the redemption, the place where God shows up in the story. Because he always does. Even in the darkest places, when the lights were out and we didn't even know him yet, he was there already.

With love, as we're ready, at just the right times, with great kindness, God shines light into our souls so we can see what's been hidden mystery to us. I see this again and again in my life, and as I sit with people hearing their stories. A woman in her sixties shares her story of sexual abuse from childhood. The shame of abuse that happened decades ago hinders intimacy with her husband today. As we pray, we ask God to shine his light and invite him to be present with that little girl. As he shows up in the story, he speaks the truth that undoes the shame. She is not dirty. It is not her fault. Love comes in with light in the past and present together, shame dissolves, and she's released into a new level of intimacy with her husband.

God comes to tell us the truth about our stories. The truth we've missed. Because so often these things happen in the early years of life. And we interpret the things that happen to us from our child perspective. We don't yet have adult eyes to see from a more grown-up point of view. In the light, God is present to reveal the false, and to root us in the love and grace that have been there the whole time.

I can tell you so many sacred stories like these—and others not like these at all. Each encounter is unique to the person, to the story. It's beautiful and holy to witness. This is the power of light exposing truth. God present with us, in us, to engage our true self. To remind us who we are, to carry us out of shame into the light, back into connection with love.

LISTENING FOR LIGHT

Our story is speaking. Our true self is speaking. God is speaking. There's a whole lot of speaking going on, bringing light, bringing truth. How do we begin to hear?

Honestly, I don't always want to hear. And I'm often not listening. (Or maybe I have my fingers in my ears, because parts of the story are too hard to hear. Lalalalalalalala.) As I learn to listen to my life, to let it speak and to let God speak through it, I find the beauty. As I hold it up in the light, like a diamond, the facets sparkle. In the light, as I listen, I discover the treasure of true self that is most deeply me.

For me, the light I need to know and live more and more in the true has come (and is coming) from many places. Gifted counselors and spiritual directors. Tools like the enneagram (I'm a 4) and Myers Briggs (INFJ). Prayer. Support groups. Mentors. Safe friends and community. All have worked together over time to help me listen to my life. I can't hear the story by myself. I need others to listen with me. Outside of relationship, I will miss the larger word being spoken.

Creating space, holding space for one another—safe, sacred spaces where we can share our stories—this is so much of the work of healing. Freedom comes to us as our words hit the light, as others listen and receive the gift of ourselves. Freedom comes to others, too. Because our stories, the spoken words of our lives, have power.

Life-mapping has also been a helpful listening tool, a way to shine light on the larger narrative of my life. Google "life-mapping" and you'll find numerous ways to put your life on paper for reflection. In my first experience, I began with a legal-sized sheet of paper turned sideways. I drew a horizonal line midway down the sheet, all the way across the page. Then I created a timeline, beginning at birth to the far left, placing marks on the line to represent each year. Slowly and prayerfully, I began to fill in the timeline of my life with events. Moved to Lexington. Moved to McAllen. Moved to North Webster. College in Nashville. Moved to Cincinnati. Jobs. Events. Relationships. Marriage. Children. South Africa. Cancer. The page began to fill.

The events that were positive, I placed above the line. The more positive, the higher it went on the page. The events that were negative, I placed below the line. The more negative, the lower it went on the page. When I was done, I began to connect the dots from left to right, graphing my life. The line went up and down, higher, then lower, then higher again.

In the end, the picture of my life included hills, mountains and valleys. Some flatline seasons. Joy. Sorrow. Successes. Failures. My journey, all there on the page like a roadmap. I could see connections and patterns and blessings I'd missed. Sadness leading to new joys. Heartache opening the way to new adventures. There with everything out in the light, the good and bad together, God began to speak my story to me. He knew things about my life I'd missed. In some of my favorite moments, I saw themes, like the joy of seeing people restored. In some of my least favorite moments, I began to see redemption.

This was my story, still very much in process. Listening led the way to acceptance. Acceptance opened the way to gratitude. And gratitude opened the floodgates for grace to come in. Not that I would have asked for the stuff below the line mind you. Who would ask for that? And not because it all feels resolved (because it doesn't). There is still pain to heal, forgiveness to release, anger to vent, and so many questions. But this is my story, and every moment of it is grace. God has been present in all of it, and I am grateful.

Gratitude practiced, over time, brings light into our story. This, says Thomas Merton, is what makes all the difference.

> To be grateful is to recognize the Love of God in every-thing He has given us—and He has given us everything. Every breath we draw is a gift of His love, every moment of existence is a grace, for it brings with it immense graces from Him. Gratitude therefore takes nothing for granted, is never unresponsive, is constantly awakening to new wonder and to praise of the goodness of God. For the grateful person knows that God is good, not by hearsay but by experience.[4]

REMEMBRANCE

Apparently the ancient Hebrews had to be reminded a lot. Read Psalm 118. It's a theme. Remember, people, God's love endures. Through it all. As you wander around in the desert eating manna every morning, his love endures. As you battle enemies, his love endures. Remember what he's done. Remember who he is. His love endures.

> Give thanks to the LORD, for he is good;
>   his love endures forever.
> Let Israel say:
>   "His love endures forever."
> Let the house of Aaron say:
>   "His love endures forever."
> Let those who fear the LORD say:
>   "His love endures forever."[5]

This refrain repeats throughout the book of Psalms. A call to remember. Because life was not easy for this small nation. Enslaved by Egyptians. Wandering in the dessert for forty years. Then entering the land promised to them, only to be repeatedly attacked by enemies. Good kings. Bad kings. Being a people chosen by God has not meant an easy life. Yet again and again, they'd seen the goodness of God. The God who was present in cloud and fire, leading, protecting, loving. They needed to be reminded of this, to remember this a lot. And so do I.

After forty years of waiting, camping, and walking in the desert, the Israelites were finally about to cross the Jordan River into the Promised Land.[6] God, in true parting-the-Red-Sea fashion, literally piles the water up upstream, and the people cross on dry ground. This seems memorable, right? A miracle like this surely the people would remember. They would talk about it all the time. Yet God directs them to set up a remembrance—twelve stones for the twelve tribes of Israel.

The Israelites made it a practice to build memorials like this one. Places of remembrance that reminded the people of their story. Reminders of the times God had done remarkable, saving, rescuing kinds of things for them. Jesus gave us a practice of remembrance, too, in communion. "Do this in remembrance of me." It seems we humans need physical, tangible reminders. Because we forget that God and grace are active and present. We forget the times that grace has shown up in our stories. Or at least I do. I forget it all the time.

Memorials—whether they be stones, journal entries, life maps, or bread and wine—help build a history of trust. And this trust becomes with time our guidance system, the window through which we see the world. The window through which we can see our stories.

As I hold my story in the light, looking for the signs of grace, I can see the saving and rescuing moments. These places of remembrance remind me, I am deeply, constantly loved. And my story of love is still being spoken. The places in my life that feel like endings are in some way beginnings. Every choice has been covered. Everything has been granted. All is grace. Remember.

HINDSIGHT

God is working in the unseen in ways we may not see for months. Or years. Or ever. He's pruning and mining the gold in our souls, deepening relationship and trust. But all we feel, all we know today, is the pain. And yet he invites us, even in this unseen place, to trust.

Moses and the Israelites were distressed.[7] So Moses heads to the tent of meeting, the place where he alone could meet with God face to face. God spoke with Moses there as one speaks to a friend. The conversation is direct and honest and real. Moses reminds God of his promises to his people, to take them into the land promised. Then Moses asks for specifics. God, you've asked me to lead this people, but you haven't shown me who you'll send with us. How will this impossible thing happen?

God promises his presence will go with them and he will give them rest. Awesome. But this doesn't seem to help Moses much, so he asks for reassurance. God responds, "I will do the very thing you have asked, because I am pleased with you and I know you by name." Sounds good, right? But Moses wants more. He makes a big, audacious ask. "Now show me your glory."

The Lord responds, offering Moses hindsight. God will cause his goodness, his presence, to pass before Moses, but Moses will only see God's back—literally, his hind side. "When my glory passes by, I will put you in a cleft in the rock and cover you with my hand until I have passed by. Then I will remove my hand and you will see my back; but my face must not be seen." This is all for Moses' good, because no one can see the full glory of the Lord and live.

Moses sees God only in hindsight, only from the back. Some rabbinical scholars interpret this to mean that we see where God has been present only after the fact. We see the presence of his shadow as we look back on our lives. This is hindsight 20/20. We see in retrospect how God has been present in the darkness, in the stress, in the mess, in the lowest points when the promise is not yet fulfilled because he's been covering our eyes. Protecting us so we are not blinded by the light of his glory, present with us in ways we can't yet know. And when he removes his hand, we see his back and know he has been with us. We have never been alone. "But maybe," writes Ann Voskamp, "this is the true reality: It is in the dark that God is passing by. The bridge and our lives shake not because God has abandoned, but the exact opposite: God is passing by. God is in the tremors. Dark is the holiest ground, the glory passing by."[8]

Is it possible that all really does work together for good? Every choice. Every turn. Not that everything that happens to us is good, or that we don't have choices we regret. We've experienced the bad first-hand. At times we've been relentlessly pummeled by it. But some-how, as we celebrate the feast of love, as we break the bread and drink the wine, we remember our story is a story of grace told in love. We remember his love endures forever.

Again, from Brené Brown: "When we deny the story, it defines us. When we own the story, we can write a brave new ending."[9] The words of our lives are still being spoken, by God and by us. And we get to write the ending. The story isn't over. What if the very best part is still to come?

DEEPER (IN)

> Every moment and every event of every man's life on earth plants something in his soul.
>
> —Thomas Merton[10]

Map Your Life

Create your own life map. You can use the process I described in this chapter. Or Google "life map" to find another approach. I love the resources available from oneLifemaps.com. Make this your own. You might paint or illustrate your journey, put sticky notes on a wall, create a poster. It's up to you.

Begin with a few moments of silence. Ask Holy Spirit to remind you of things that are important. Take your time.

When you've created your map, take some time to reflect. What stands out to you? What connections do you see? Patterns? Themes? Directional changes? What have you overcome? Where do you see joy? When has God been most present to you?

Ask Holy Spirit to enlighten your map. Where has God been present in your journey? Where have you not yet met God in your story? What is he inviting you to today?

Respond to God's invitation to you. You might also journal anything that feels important.

CHAPTER 11

◆

(IN) Darkness

Someone I loved once gave me a box full of darkness.
It took me years to understand that this, too, was a gift.
—MARY OLIVER[1]

YOU CAN'T REALLY GO through cancer, as someone who prays for healing, without taking a good, hard look inside. And I did. Lord, is there a root? Unforgiveness? Anger? Anything? Please just show me. I want to deal with it. It turned out I did have some anger. OK, maybe a lot. At my dad. Whom I'd forgiven in part, but not in full.

Forgiveness is a process more than an event. Small seeds of bitterness were still hidden in my soul, and the Lord kindly revealed them. Did the cancer grow from these seeds? I have no idea. The things we hold in our souls can make our bodies sick. But I'll never really know for sure if the bitterness and cancer were connected. Either way, I was free of them and healed at a deeper level. I'd done the work of healing. I'd walked through cancer openly and honestly, sharing the journey. I had, I thought, done it well with Jesus. Overachiever, take a bow.

So when, five years later, my mammogram revealed another tumor, I was, honestly, pissed. I'd been planning a five-year cancer-free party. He said I'd be healed, right? Seriously, God. We did this already. And I thought I did it pretty well. The bitterness is gone. So why is this happening again?

I'd never really asked the "why" question the first time. After all, why *not* me? Following Jesus does not give us a get-out-of-suffering-free pass, despite what some would lead us to believe. The sin and pain and evil of the world leave plenty of room for suffering. And I believe, really believe, that God redeems it all. It's one of my favorite things about him. Beauty for ashes, every time.

But now I was asking why. And loudly—at least loudly to God. I was disappointed, angry, and ashamed. By now, I was leading a prayer ministry and a lot of eyes were on me. And I knew at least some of them were judging. Twice? Really? There must be some unresolved issue, some reason, some hidden sin. I knew they were thinking it because I'd been tempted to think this about others. This, it turns out, is not what love does.

So again, many gathered around and prayed as we moved through the diagnosis and decisions about treatment. Treatment options I did not like at all. And this time, several trusted voices said they believed I would receive the instantaneous miracle. I would be a sign and a wonder. I believed God spoke this to me as well. So I stood in the promise. Publicly. And we prayed in community for my healing.

It turns out, when God said I would have to go all the way, he meant it. Even five years later, he meant it. And "all the way" was a double mastectomy. I did not want it. I wanted the miracle. I searched and cried out for the why. What do I need to repent of? Who do I need to forgive? All I heard was, "You have an enemy. This is from him." That did not help very much.

When instantaneous healing eluded me, I went silent. Into hiding. I moved from angry to ashamed. I didn't want to be seen or judged. I didn't trust the love of God or others, not in this season. The recovery felt long and hard and dark. My body was forever changed. I hated the scars.

Weeks after treatment was complete, I stood in front of the mirror, looking at the scars across my chest. Crying hard. Feeling the shame of the disfigurement I couldn't escape in my body and my soul. And suddenly, Jesus was there. I don't know how to explain this to you. I just know he was there in the most tangible kind of way I've ever experienced. Not in a physical, audible kind of way, but in a way that felt every bit as real.

Eyes filled with quiet compassion, he extended his hands, lifting them so I could see his scars. I heard the words he spoke quietly in my soul, "I understand." The knowing of his love went deep in a moment. He did understand the pain of scars. Of loss. Of death. Of disfigurement. And he knew the redemption they bring. He brought redemption to me that day. His truth broke the power of the shame. When I look at my scars now, I see his scars. Beauty for ashes. That's what he does. All the time.

WRESTLING IN THE DARK

In the Gospels, Jesus and his friends are healing and saving and delivering with the simplest of prayers. And as someone who prays with people for healing, I get to see this, too. Sometimes. But when I don't see the same thing happening in my life, in the way I hope and expect, disappointment begins to win. Hope is deferred. My heart becomes sick. And darkness moves in.

Cancer made more than my body sick. The disappointment, the hope deferred, made my heart sick. I've prayed, right? God is good, right? So why is the bad still here, staring me in the face, breathing down my neck, disfiguring my body? Why am I still sick? From our disappointment and darkness, the timeless, unanswerable question emerges. Why?

It's a really valid question. And I don't think God minds it at all. He values our honesty and operates in the real. And he almost always answers it with an invitation: Trust me. I'm with you. I will never leave you. Remain. Abide. The life and light you seek are here.

And that helps. A little. Sometimes.

Disappointment leaves us in the dark, bumping into questions with no easy answers. It challenges what we believe about God. About ourselves. And this challenge, this is good. Because in the challenge, God invites us to wrestle. And in the wrestling, in the encounter, we find the blessing.

Jacob was up against it.[2] He was about to meet Esau, the brother he'd betrayed, stealing his birthright. He'd sent lavish gifts ahead, and all he knew was that his brother was coming to meet him. With four hundred men. It was night. Jacob was scared. And right in the middle of the night and the fear, God comes to wrestle. They wrestle until dawn, and Jacob refuses to let go without a blessing. So God gives him a limp and a new name. "Your name will no longer be Jacob, but Israel, because you have struggled with God and with humans and have overcome." The identity of a man and of a nation are established through a long night of wrestling and the blessing given at dawn. And so it is with us.

We wrestle in the night with big questions. God, are you really good? Are you even paying attention? Do you love me? Have I done something wrong? I think God welcomes the questions, because they open the door to conversation, to connection, to encounter. Through the questions, the tears, the cursing, the yelling, we wrestle. We get close, we get raw, we get real. And God comes, present to heal and bless in a way we never expected.

Madam Guyon was a seventeenth-century French mystic, a woman who loved God and experienced his presence in prayer in ways that were very unsettling to the church folk in her day. She operated outside the religious box with God, and I tend to like that a lot in a person. One day, reading one of her books on prayer, her encounter became mine as well. I'd had cancer twice. And God had done no supernatural, instantaneous healing. And I was a little upset with him. We've already established this.

Madam Guyon had been sick. For a long time. And she'd been

asking God to heal her with no visible results. The sickness remained. And one day, she decided to pray differently. She stopped asking God to heal her and started asking for an encounter with the God who heals.

This is big, people. This is trust. This is a prayer answered every time. In her darkness, she did not question God's character. She changed her pursuit. Instead of pursuing healing, she determined to pursue the God whose very character and nature is healing. The God whose very character and nature is good. She determined to pursue his presence, an encounter with the living God. She took her place (IN) him, recognizing his presence (IN) her, choosing to remain in his love.

She knew God to be good. Nothing she had experienced changed that. She also knew that an encounter with God brought another kind of healing, the transformation, the making whole of our whole selves, soul and spirit. The becoming of our true selves. He doesn't cause the pain and sickness (not ever). He meets us in it. Every time.

NECESSARY PARTNERS

The encounters that change our names and our prayers seem to come most often in the darkness of night. In sickness, in loss, in addiction, in desperation. And walking (or wrestling) in this dark feels scary. I can't see where I'm going. Or what I might bump in to. Or who else might be in the room with me. I prefer light, definitely. I can see where I'm going. I can feel like I'm in control. No surprises. Cancer, both times, felt like a long walk down a dank, dark cavern in the company of pain, fear, loss, unknowing, anger, shame. My partners in the journey were real and present. The dark was real and present. And yet, in the darkness, my partners were transformed. And I became more me.

In the classic tale *Hinds' Feet on High Places*,[3] little Much Afraid journeys from the Valley of Fearings to the high places at the invitation of the Good Shepherd. Her feet are crooked and her legs are weak, so the Shepherd gives her two companions to help—Sorrow and Suffering.

Much Afraid fears these companions (as she fears everything), but she soon learns she must lean on them if she is to make the long journey from the valley into the mountains.

It's a beautiful story, and it feels very much like my story every time I read it. Through injury, dangers, setbacks, and so much fear, Much Afraid finally arrives at the High Places. There in the Kingdom of Love, Much Afraid is transformed and the true identity of her companions is revealed. Sorrow and Suffering have been Joy and Peace all along. And Much Afraid has always been Grace-and-Glory. She just didn't know it yet. The knowing of herself and the growing trust in the goodness of her Shepherd required this long climb. And her companions Sorrow and Suffering were essential. She would not have made it to the summit without them.

God gives us companions in our journeys we would not choose for ourselves. I would never choose the dark of cancer. But I would never trade the gifts it's given me. In the darkness, in the company of sorrow and suffering, I found the true. I learned trust. I discovered joy and peace. And I emerged more fully me. "Joy and pain," writes Ann Voskamp, "they are but two arteries of the one heart that pumps through all those who don't numb themselves to really living."[4]

The apostle Paul said it this way in his letter to the Corinthians:

> For God, who said, "Let light shine out of darkness," made his light shine in our hearts to give us the light of the knowledge of God's glory displayed in the face of Christ.
>
> But we have this treasure in jars of clay to show that this all-surpassing power is from God and not from us. We are hard pressed on every side, but not crushed; perplexed, but not in despair; persecuted, but not abandoned; struck down, but not destroyed. We always carry around in our body the death of Jesus, so that the life of Jesus may also be revealed in our body. For we who are alive are always being

given over to death for Jesus' sake, so that his life may also
be revealed in our mortal body. So then, death is at work in
us, but life is at work in you. . . .

Therefore we do not lose heart. Though outwardly we
are wasting away, yet inwardly we are being renewed day by
day. For our light and momentary troubles are achieving for
us an eternal glory that far outweighs them all. So we fix our
eyes not on what is seen, but on what is unseen, since what is
seen is temporary, but what is unseen is eternal.[5]

Cancer made me very aware that death was at work in my body. I
was literally wasting away. The pressing was hard. I felt like I was being
crushed. But even in this darkness, light was present. I carried light
unseen in me. Treasure, eternal glory, in a cracked pot. God present
(IN) me, with me, in the darkness. Not in a way I could see or sense. But
in a way that sustained. In a way that renewed daily, coming like manna
in the desert.

We are invited by a Good Shepherd to journey in the company of
Sorrow and Suffering. This journey into fullness of life requires a
death. And in this place, the last place we would expect it or can feel
it, we find the eternal light that lives in us. The light that has been
and will always be. This light is how we navigate in the dark.

> Is there any place I can go to avoid your Spirit?
> to be out of your sight?
> If I climb to the sky, you're there!
> If I go underground, you're there!
> If I flew on morning's wings
> to the far western horizon,
> You'd find me in a minute—
> you're already there waiting!
> Then I said to myself, "Oh, he even sees me in the dark!

At night I'm immersed in the light!"
It's a fact: darkness isn't dark to you;
  night and day, darkness and light, they're all the same
to you.[6]

Darkness and light are the same to God. Because he is present in both. And both are needed. In the beginning, light came in darkness. In the way of Jesus, resurrection came in tomb. He does not save me from the darkness. He saves me in the darkness.

Very truly I tell you, unless a kernel of wheat falls to the ground and dies, it remains only a single seed. But if it dies, it produces many seeds. Anyone who loves their life will lose it, while anyone who hates their life in this world will keep it for eternal life.[7]

This is probably not what you were hoping to hear from Jesus. And really, I wish there was another way. A quick prayer or two. And maybe a puppy or kitten, because that would be lovely. But fullness of life requires a willingness to yield ourselves, to remove all that hinders, to submit to love. It's the death that makes room for life, for new. It's no easy ask. Jesus asked his Father to take the cup of death away. It's no surprise when we shrink back, afraid of what the freedom will cost. Afraid of encountering our pain, of feeling it, being present to it in order to find God with us in it. But when we give our yes, just as he did, the rising begins. Thomas Kelly writes:

For if you will accept as normal life only what you can understand, then you will try only to expel the dull, dead weight of Destiny, of inevitable suffering which is a part of normal life, and never come to terms with it or fit your soul to the collar and bear the burden of your suffering which must be borne by you, or enter into the divine education and drastic discipline of sorrow, or rise radiant in the sacrament of pain.[8]

IT TAKES TWO HANDS

Life is a mixed bag. Good and bad together. Light and dark. Color and shadow. Healing and suffering. It's hard to hold them both at the same time. To accept them both. I want the good, the parts that feel like blessing and favor. I'll pass on the bad, thank you very much, because it feels . . . well, just awful. I tend to hold the good out front for all to see, and I tend to hide the bad because it can look pretty ugly. And who wants to see that?

I think I do this in part because I'm judging myself—and maybe also, judging God. The bad means I'm bad. Unloved. It means somehow I've missed the cut when it comes to protection and blessing and favor. The bad means there must be something wrong.

But what if both good and bad, both light and dark, are here not by merit, but in grace? What if it's about learning to live rooted and grounded in love in both? Maybe both have something to offer me and the world. Maybe. Because I really wish it were another way. A blessing-filled, comfortable, easy-breezy-beachy kind of way. And it's this wish, this expectation, that opens wide the door to disappointment.

When we equate only blessing with the love of God, when we insist on the quick and easy answers, the immediate healing, the microwave solution, we miss the mercy. We want, sometimes even demand, prevention. God promises presence. In the dark night of the soul, we encounter an essential grace.

St. John of the Cross experienced the dark night as a wilderness of disconnection from God. A time of purging, stripping, emptying. And this night, said John, is essential to the union of the soul with God. Through the dark night, the "root of the imperfection and impurity" is removed and we are led to a higher degree of love.[9]

In her book *Learning to Walk in the Darkness*, Barbara Brown Taylor writes this about St. John's dark night:

> [T]he dark night is God's best gift to you, intended for your liberation. It is about freeing you from your ideas about God, your fears about God, your attachment to all the benefits you have been promised for believing in God, your devotion to the spiritual practices that are supposed to make you feel closer to God, your dedication to doing and believing all the right things about God, your positive and negative evaluations of yourself as a believer in God, your tactics for manipulating God, and your sure cures for doubting God.[10]

In the darkness, we are dismantled, deconstructed, and freed to live in a more open, spacious place with God. Here we have less certainty—and more deep knowing. Here we encounter God on his terms, and find there's more light and more love than we'd ever imagined. In St. John's own words, "No soul will ever grow deep in the spiritual life unless God works passively in that soul by means of the dark night."

LESS IS MORE

Our dismantling, the pruning of the soul, is mercy. Only with pruning can we live rooted and remaining in love.

> I am the true vine, and my Father is the gardener. He cuts off every branch in me that bears no fruit, while every branch that does bear fruit he prunes so that it will be even more fruitful. You are already clean because of the word I have spoken to you. Remain in me, as I also remain in you. No branch can bear fruit by itself; it must remain in the vine.

Neither can you bear fruit unless you remain in me. I am the
vine; you are the branches. If you remain in me and I in you,
you will bear much fruit; apart from me you can do nothing.[11]

When I hear the words of Jesus, I don't hear the mercy. At least
not at first. It feels violent to me, the cutting and the pruning. And
yet every vineyard worker, every gardener, knows that the life of the
vine, the flourishing and all the fruit, depends on pruning.

In these verses, the apostle John uses a word for "cuts off" that
has three meanings: to raise up, to carry, and to remove. He's giving us a gentle picture of an attentive gardener, lifting the vine and
placing it in the light where it can be restored. In this picture the
gardener is working to remove the things that hinder love to open
the flow of life and healing. In this picture I find mercy.

I experience the pruning—the removing, cleansing, healing
work of Spirit in me—so often as a death. But the real death is in the
disconnection—the shame, the pain, the disappointment that leaves
me separated from God, from myself, from others. All of life is
nourished in the life-flow of connection, in relationship, in friendship with Jesus.

"My command is this: Love each other as I have loved you. Greater
love has no one than this: to lay down one's life for one's friends. You
are my friends if you do what I command."[12]

This friendship with Jesus requires a laying down of our lives.
Of our right to be right, to be healed, to be safe. As Jesus laid down
his life, trusting his Father, he invites us to do the same. Because in
the laying down, in the very thing that feels like the end, we find the
beginning. And through the intimacy of friendship, we encounter
the greatest love.

This love, this light, the presence of God, dwells (IN) us. We carry
within us all we need for life, all we need for love, all we need to know
ourselves and God. We do not need more. We need less. We need the

mercy of the pruning. The roots that have gone down in pain and disappointment and in practices and beliefs that do not bring life, these roots need to be removed. The pruning work of subtraction opens space within us for the new. Rooted ever more deeply in love, we experience union, the union God intended from the very beginning. Thomas Merton writes:

> Tribulation detaches us from the things of nothingness in which we spend ourselves and die. Therefore, tribulation gives us life, not out of love for death, but out of love for life. Let me then withdraw all my love from scattered, vain things—the desire to be read and praised as a writer, to be a successful teacher praised by my students, or to live at ease in some beautiful place—and let me place everything in thee, where it will take root and live, instead of being spent in barrenness.[13]

DEEPER (IN)

Giving thanks is that: making the canyon of pain into a megaphone to proclaim the ultimate goodness of God when Satan and all the world would sneer at us to recant.
—Ann Voskamp[14]

Gratitude is a powerful way to find and see God in our darkness. In the coming week, choose one of these activities to practice gratitude.

Gratitude Journal

For the next seven days, keep an eye out for things you are thankful for. Ask God to highlight people, places, events. At the end of each day, take several quiet moments with God to reflect. Ask for hindsight. Then, list ten things from the day you are thankful for. Offer a prayer of thanks.

Finding Light in the Dark

Prayerfully reflect with God on a time of darkness in your past. As you look back, how do you see God? How was he present in that time? How were you changed? How was your view of God changed? Write a short prayer of thanksgiving to God.

CHAPTER 12

◆

(IN) Sight

After all, the true seeing is within.
—GEORGE ELIOT[1]

I AM CONSTANTLY AMAZED at the courage of the people who come to the Roots&Branches prayer room. Their bravery is a beautiful trust. They are seeking healing, relief from pain, release from stuck places in their lives. Usually, they've already tried a lot of things. Maybe they've sought deliverance from a spirit holding them captive. Maybe they've taken medication. Fasted. Tried essential oils. Maybe they've been to counseling. They've read, prayed, memorized, meditated. And some, maybe all, of these things have helped, because these *can* all be helpful things. But still the pain, the shame is there—the stuck place that leaves them disconnected from God, from themselves, from others. So they've gotten a little desperate. And in their desperation, they've become brave enough to trust two strangers to sit with them, to hear their story, and to listen with them to God. And this desperation, this willingness to bring the pain and shame into the light, opens the door to encounter that heals.

My partner and I were scheduled to meet with a young married man. And I already didn't like him. I didn't like him at all. (This, by the way, is not a helpful attitude for a prayer room leader.) He'd told us on his intake form that he'd been cheating on his wife and lying. And I'd already formed lots of opinions about him on behalf of his wife.

Realizing this would not be helpful to this man or to his session, I released my judgments to God as we prayed before we met with him. Without love in the room, nothing good would happen. We all do the things we do for a reason. This young man had a story, and he needed to meet God right in the middle of it.

James (not his real name) was tired of all the lying. He couldn't carry the weight anymore. The lies, which had started early in life, were taking a toll on him and on all his relationships. As we listened, making safe space for him to bring his story into the light, he told us his affair was only the most recent of his lies. From early on, this gifted young man had been failing intentionally and lying about it. He would fail in school and find a way to cover it up. He'd dropped out of college but told everyone he'd graduated. He'd secretly gone back to college to try to finish his degree, had dropped out again, and had kept it all secret. Now everyone wondered why he was so underemployed. He was feeling pressure to get a higher-paying job but couldn't without a degree. He'd sabotaged his education, his career, and now his marriage. He was having an affair, and he'd told his wife. The affair for him was a way out, a way to fail at this marriage and get out from under all the lies. James was disconnected from God, from himself, and from his wife. His self-sabotaging choices were costing him everything.

James wanted to know what was causing this painful pattern in his life. So we invited Holy Spirit to begin to open this up with him. We asked Spirit to give James a safe place to meet with Jesus, to encounter him, to see and hear from him. As James began to feel more peace, he sensed a connection. God was present to him. We asked Holy Spirit to show James when this pattern started for him, when he first began to believe he needed to lie, to hide. Then we waited.

James said a memory came to mind, something he hadn't thought of for years, from preschool or maybe kindergarten. It was winter. All the children were outside playing in the snow at recess. Some of them were throwing their hats against the side of the school building, and the hats were sticking in the snow and ice. It became a game. Who could throw their hat the highest? James won. His hat went so high he couldn't reach it to get it down. When the teacher came to bring them back to class, she screamed at James. In front of the whole class. James was frozen, there in the snow, with fear. As we asked the Lord to heal the trauma that little boy had experienced, we asked Holy Spirit what that little boy believed in that moment. There in the light, James listened and new understanding came. A connection he'd never seen before. "I decided it wasn't safe to be the best. That I would never be the best again because I would get in trouble." This belief, rooted in James' memory, in his soul, was the lie that was shaping his life as an adult.

We kept going. "Jesus, this little boy believes it isn't safe to be the best. That he'll get in trouble. What do you say?" James, still connected with his experience in the memory, aware of his teacher and the other students, looked for Jesus. James saw Jesus come pull the hat down off the building, then walk to the little boy. Jesus gave him back his hat with a smile, and told him he thought it was great that James could throw his hat so high. He gave James a hug and let him know it was OK to be him, to succeed. It was safe.

In that place of trauma, James encountered Jesus. He was stunned. He had no idea his self-destructive behaviors had anything to do with the shame and trauma he'd experienced on the playground. James turned from the lie to the truth as we prayed. And in that turning, James was becoming rooted in a new, more true way of seeing and knowing himself.

BEFRIENDING OUR PAIN

The most holy thing I do, if I do anything holy at all, is to sit with people in their pain. Just sit. Like Job's friends did, sitting in *shiva*, the silent "being with." It was the best thing they did—far better than all the talking. In fact, God takes them to task for the talking—because the talking was about trying to make Job's pain make sense. And there was no making sense of it, from a human perspective. Job's pain was about a deal made in an unseen place, and God trusting Job so much that he put everything but Job's life on the line. As the story goes, God gave the Accuser access to all of Job's life, save his breath. And the Accuser had taken it all.

Job's friends wanted to make it make sense. Surely Job had done something wrong, had lost favor with God. But this wasn't the case, not at all. Job makes his case honestly before God. He has done nothing to deserve this, yet he's been abandoned, crushed. Job asks the question, makes the accusation we've all made at some point, at the darkest point: "I cry out to you, God, but you do not answer; I stand up, but you merely look at me. You turn on me ruthlessly; with the might of your hand you attack me."[2]

Job speaks from his pain honestly, directly. He holds nothing back. And neither does God, who is not about to explain himself to Job nor to anyone else. He answers Job from the storm with a very long series of questions on a theme: Who are you, Job, to question me? God has a lot to say at this point about who he is. In the end, Job realizes he hadn't known God at all. "Surely I spoke of things I did not understand, things too wonderful for me to know."[3]

Job had lived faithfully for God, but he'd not yet encountered God. Only here, in his honest, raw pain, had he come face to face. "My ears had heard of you but now my eyes have seen you."[4] In this place of encounter, Job turns. He repents and retracts his words and conceptions about God. Job realizes he is made from dust, so he returns to dust and ashes in repentance. From this face to face experience of knowing, from encounter and dust, "the LORD blessed the latter days of Job more than his beginning."[5] Yes, God restored Job's stuff, but the stuff is not the point. The knowing is the point. It is in seeing, in encounter, we experience, we know, we are restored. And our latter days become more than our beginning.

The pain of Job's life was an invitation to encounter, to a greater knowing of God and of himself. Our pain is an invitation, too. A call to wake up and listen to our lives. What if, instead of avoiding the pain with food or reality TV or alcohol or toxic relationships or any of the other ways we try to numb or fill, we said yes to the invitation to encounter? "What if," asks Barbara Brown Taylor, "I could learn to trust my feelings instead of asking to be delivered from them? What if I could follow one of my great fears all the way to the edge of the abyss, take a breath, and keep going? Isn't there a chance of being surprised by what happens next?"[6]

I am stunned again and again by the beauty revealed in my own life and in the lives of others as we walk up to the edge of the abyss, take that deep breath, and keep going together. Because the pain shows us the way to our healing. Again from Barbara Brown Taylor, "There is no filling a hole that was never designed to be filled, but only to be entered into."[7]

"My own experience with anguish," writes Henri Nouwen, "has been that facing it and living it through is the way to healing. But I cannot do it on my own. I need someone to keep me standing in it, to assure me that there is peace beyond the anguish, life beyond death and love beyond fear. But I know now, at least, that attempting to avoid, repress or escape the pain is like cutting off a limb that could be healed with proper attention."[8]

SEEING IS BELIEVING

Our experiences and the learnings associated with them—what we've seen, felt, tasted, touched, smelled—are held in our brains and bodies. Narratives held together in memory, good and bad, true and false, together. The memories we hold from ages three and five and twelve, and yesterday, continue to speak both truth and lies today. For me, the smell of coffee is still connected with the decades-old memory of the burnt coffee in my mom's percolator. Today I can only drink coffee tasting mostly like chocolate. A voice raised in anger today is still sometimes connected with the memory of my father's yelling, and I feel angry and frozen and in trouble all over again. These sensory narratives are strong and lasting. They form our beliefs, drive our choices, and shape our lives. To see (or smell or taste or touch) really is to believe.

To believe something different, we need to see and experience something different. As we encounter God in our pain, as we find him present in our past, we see what is true. We see the unseen that's been true the whole time. In seeing and experiencing Jesus present in the pain, our memories, beliefs, and emotions are healed.

Our capacity to see (hear, taste, feel) our past experiences, and to encounter Jesus there, is housed in our imagination. This place in our brain has the power to reproduce and change images stored in memory. I think of the imagination as the part of my brain that operates in pictures, a canvas God paints on, showing me my past, present, and future as he sees and knows it. The imagination is the place of visions, dreams, and the seeing of seers. This is the place of beholding.

"Now the Lord is the Spirit, and where the Spirit of the Lord is, there is freedom. And we all, who with unveiled faces contemplate the Lord's glory, are being transformed into his image with ever-increasing glory, which comes from the Lord, who is the Spirit."[9] It is this beholding, the seeing, that changes us.

As we see what's true about us, about our story, about God, we are transformed more and more into his image, more and more into our true selves. Greg Boyd, in his book *Seeing Is Believing*, writes:

> If our faith is going to be powerful and transformative, it is going to have to be imaginative and experiential. St. Ignatius, founder of the Jesuits, wrote, "It is not knowing a lot but grasping things intimately and savoring them that fills and satisfies the soul." Memories shape us profoundly

because we grasp them and savor them not as information but "intimately."[10]

I know intimately through encounter. Through an experience with God that fills and satisfies my soul. This is the place where Jesus becomes real to me. Where I see and begin to believe differently. Where the truth about me, about God, about everything comes to life. And this is the whole point. "You can actually encounter the living Christ," writes Richard Foster, "be addressed by his voice and be touched by his healing power. It can be more than an exercise of the imagination. It can be a confrontation. Jesus Christ will actually come to you."[11]

MEETING JESUS JUST IN TIME

The Pharisees came into the temple with a woman.[12] She had been caught in the act of adultery. Now she is humiliated, publicly exposed, shamed. According to the Law, she should be stoned with the man she had been with. Except the Pharisees don't seem to be worried about the man at all. He's nowhere to be found. They've brought the woman to use her to trap Jesus. "Jesus, the law tells us to stone a woman like this. What do you say?"

Jesus is brilliant. He's not drawn into a theological debate. He knows what they're up to. He bends down and writes on the ground with his finger. I've always wondered what he wrote. I'd love to know. Maybe "Thou shalt not kill" in Hebrew. Whatever it was, it unsettled the Pharisees. They keep questioning, trying to draw Jesus in. He finally stands up and says (brilliantly), "Let any one of you who is without sin be the first to throw a stone at her." Then he stoops down and continues writing. All the while, the woman watches, waits, her fate in the hands of this man bent before her.

Slowly the crowd disperses, the older ones first, then the younger, until only Jesus and the woman remain. Jesus straightens up and asks her, "Where are they? Has no one condemned you?"

"No one," she replies.

"Then neither do I condemn you. Go now and leave your life of sin."

The only one present who could have cast that stone chose the law of love. The greatest commandment. And, perhaps for the first time, this woman was with a man who did not use her. Perhaps for the first time, she looked into the eyes of a man who did not judge or abuse or shame. She encountered love that bent before her to write on her behalf. A kind love that forgives. In this encounter with Jesus, in this new seeing, she was released to live a new way. A word, a touch, a look from Jesus heals. This is the power of encounter.

We're invited to encounter Jesus just as this woman did. Not in flesh, but fully in Spirit. Jesus reveals himself present with us in our shame. He's always been there. He has never left us, never deserted. He has wept with us. Been angry on our behalf. Grieved our loss. And protected in ways we'd not seen or known. He knows the lies shame has told us. And he knows the truth. In the place of encounter, he opens the eyes of our imagination to see what was unseen and unknown, and to tell us what's true. As we see and experience the new, the old self-defensive, self-protective, self-destructive patterns fall away. We are renewed to live in the true. From John Eldredge:

> He wants truth in our inmost being, and to get it there he's got to take us into our inmost being. One way he'll do this is by bringing up an old memory. You'll be driving down the road and suddenly remember something from your childhood. Or maybe you'll have a dream about a long-forgotten person, event or place. However he brings it up, go with him there. He has something to say to you. . . . The lessons that have been laid down in pain can be accessed only in pain. Christ must open the wound, not just bandage it over.[13]

These encounters in memory change our stories. Or maybe it's more accurate to say they complete our stories, showing us what we hadn't seen or known at the time. The narratives that drive us, true and false, are rooted in our minds. More precisely, in our brains, the center of our thoughts, memories, emotions, and responses. The lies we believe about ourselves, about God, about our relationships, about our lives—they are all held here, in our heads. And this is the place of renewal.

We are transformed, says the apostle Paul, by the renewing of our minds. By the making new of our thoughts, memories, emotions, and responses. I used to think Paul meant I needed to know new facts—that information, repeated often enough to my brain, would change me. And sometimes it does, a little. But we're invited to more than information. We're invited to the knowing of encounter. Being told I am loved and experiencing being loved are two very different things. Again from Greg Boyd:

> Here is where the abstract truth about God's love and glory is made concrete and personalized into a transforming experience in the Spirit-inspired imagination of the believer. It is through this spiritual mental vision that we are "transformed by the renewing of our minds" (Romans 12:2) and set free from the pattern of this world.[14]

ROOTED PRAYER

Our transformation happens in the reality of what's true in our lives today. Right in the middle of the stress, anxiety, depression, fear, worry, self-doubt, unlove, the parts of us rooted in wounding and shame—this is where transformation happens. You don't have to get out of it to meet Jesus. You don't have to be some better version of yourself to meet Jesus. He wants to walk right into the middle of it and be with you. To remove the things in the way and root you in that very place in the truth of his love and presence. In the truth of your identity (IN) him. You, just as you are, in holy process.

Our overreactions, triggers, recurring painful emotions, the cycles of behavior we can't seem to break—all of these are inviting us to encounter. To a new seeing that requires safety. We need safe space with God to dare to bring these memories into the light. We need safe space with others who will hold and honor our story. Only in safety can we risk being fully seen and known.

As we sit with people to practice what we call Rooted Prayer,[15] we hold safe space together. We listen, not to question or counsel, but to open sacred space for clients to hear themselves, follow their thoughts, explore their stories. Even in the listening, healing begins. If we will hold this space long enough, simply reflecting, waiting, listening, something will shift nearly always around the twenty- to twenty-five-minute mark. Clients will make a new connection, have a flash of insight, know something about themselves they didn't know before. This listening is essential to the process.

Next we invite the client to move into a place of listening connection with God. We ask Holy Spirit to give them a safe space to meet with Jesus. We bless them to see with spiritual eyes, to hear with spiritual ears. Together, we hold a question before Jesus, and we wait to see what the client hears, sees, or senses. Where does this overreaction come from? When did they first believe the lie? How or where does Jesus want to meet them in their pain? The questions we ask are based on the story, but the questions themselves aren't that important. What's important is the space to listen.

As clients like James share what they see or hear or sense, the thoughts or images or memories that come to mind, we simply ask the next question, facilitating their encounter with God. Waiting to see what happens next. As Holy Spirit leads, we follow. Spirit together with spirit knows the way to the true. Leanne Payne writes:

We simply invoke His Presence, then invite Him into
our hearts. He shows us our hearts. In prayer for the healing of memories, we simply ask our Lord to come present to
that place where we were so wounded (or perhaps wounded
another). Forgiving others, and receiving forgiveness,
occurs. In prayer for the healing of the heart from fears,
bitterness, etc., we see primal fears as well as lesser ones
dealt with immediately: those fears that the sufferer often
has not been aware of, never been able to name—they only
know that their lives have been seriously restricted and
shaped because of them.[16]

As clients encounter Jesus, their experiences are as unique as
their stories. And they are breathtaking. The beauty of how God is
present to them, with them, of what he speaks to them, is stunning.
At this point we are on holy ground.

In every encounter, God gives an invitation: Will we release the
lie to receive the truth? Will we forgive those who have wounded us?
Will we forgive ourselves? Will we admit where we've missed the
mark? Confess where we've hurt others? Release the burdens that
aren't ours to carry? What response are we ready to make today to
the invitation? As clients respond to God's invitation, we pray with
and for them, saying no to the false and yes to the true, forgiving and
receiving forgiveness, releasing trauma and shame, commanding
darkness to go. As we listen and pray, the false is pruned and true
self is revealed. Here they are rooted in love. All because we have
been in the presence of Jesus.

And this presence is always the point. "At the day's end," writes
author and speaker Randy Clark, "healing ministry is not about
using a certain kind of model; it's about people encountering the
Healer. It's not about principles; it's about presence."[17]

DEEPER (IN)

A Rooted Prayer Experience

Where have you not yet met Jesus in your story? He's already there. You just haven't seen him yet. He's been present with you, in all of your story, in every moment of light and dark. There has never been anywhere you could go apart from his presence.

Set aside fifteen to twenty minutes of time in a quiet, comfortable space where you won't be disturbed. Turn off your phone or set it aside. Close your eyes. Take a few deep breaths. Invite God's presence. Ask Holy Spirit to enlighten your imagination. To give you eyes to see and ears to hear.

Wait for a sense of connection, a sense of God with you. If you're feeling blocked or distracted, turn your thoughts gently back to God. Ask him to remove anything in the way.

Ask God where in your story he'd like to meet you today. See what comes to mind. Is it a memory from first grade? A memory from yesterday? Hold the scene before God. Allow yourself to feel and see what's there. Then invite Jesus to show you where he is, what he's doing and feeling. Watch the scene. Where do you see him? What is he doing? How does he feel about what's happening? As he's with you, ask him what you believed about yourself (or him, or others) in this moment that isn't true. Ask him to tell you, to show you what is true.

As he shows you what's true about you, do you sense an invitation to respond in some way? To reject the lie and agree with what God says is true? Do you need to forgive someone? Or yourself? Do you need to release guilt or shame? Take time to listen, to respond, and to receive grace, truth and love in his presence.

If you're not sensing anything as you pray, that's OK. You can still dialogue with Jesus about the situation or memory that comes to mind. If at any point what you are seeing feels too overwhelming, you can ask God for a safe place to meet with him and talk. Or simply rest in a safe place in his presence.

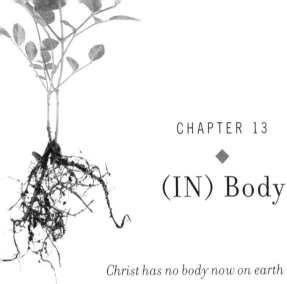

◆

CHAPTER 13

(IN) Body

Christ has no body now on earth but yours.
—TERESA OF AVILA[1]

MY HUSBAND AND I joined the Undivided journey to be part of a new racial reconciliation movement in the already very diverse megachurch we'd been attending. We knew our hearts needed to be challenged, healed, and expanded. We knew our mostly white suburban world, our circle of friends needed to be more diverse. We didn't yet know what we didn't know.

The first night, we were assigned to intentionally diverse groups of ten to twelve people. We introduced ourselves by telling why we'd chosen to be part of Undivided. I loved Keana (not her real name) right away for her honesty. She told us she didn't want to be here. She didn't want to have to try to help white people understand the black experience. She'd tried before, multiple times, and it hadn't gone well. She shared stories of fear and prejudice from life in her mostly white suburb. She was angry and tired of all of it. But she felt compelled by God to come, to be part of this. I was grateful.

Through the six-week experience, our group shared stories, fears, judgments. We learned about social, economic, and educational constructs that keep us divided. We sat around a table, drank wine, and broke bread together. We became friends.

In our last session, we were asked to consider with God where we held attitudes and judgments against people who were different from us. Then we were asked to get into groups of two, to look into another's eyes, and confess our sin. Gulp. For a second or two I considered going light on this. Taking an easier way. Then I caught Keana's eye and went all in. I asked if she would do this exercise with me.

As I looked into her eyes, I felt my heart breaking. I'd been horrified to find so much privilege there, so much that wanted to keep me separate. Through my tears, I tried to offer some words, to confess my sin. But I didn't even know how to name it. Keana knew. She looked at me with tender understanding. "You are afraid. It is fear." She knew me better than I knew myself. Her words cut kindly to bring healing. Yes, it was fear. Fear that someone having more might mean I have less. Fear that love would cost me something. And here's the thing: Love *always* costs us something. In the end, if we love well, it will cost us everything.

Keana received my confession and ministered forgiveness to my soul that night with gentleness and mercy. I offered the same to her in return. I think she gave the greater gift. In that moment, in the sacred, naked space, we were one. We were undivided.

ROOTED TOGETHER

God took on body, that we each might become his body—individual hands, feet, hearts embodying the love of Jesus. Embodying Jesus is a worthy, lifelong pursuit, no doubt. Our bodies carry Holy Spirit as temples of the presence of God. This is a big freaking deal.

But just in case you've been thinking the journey (IN) is about you, let's be clear. We are meant to live rooted together. In fact, this is the point of our life in Christ. And in the end, it is the fulfillment of all things.

> In him we have redemption through his blood, the forgiveness of sins, in accordance with the riches of God's grace

that he lavished on us. With all wisdom and understanding, he made known to us the mystery of his will according to his good pleasure, which he purposed in Christ, to be put into effect when the times reach their fulfillment—to bring unity to all things in heaven and on earth under Christ.[2]

Our (IN)-ness is about oneness—not just with God, but ultimately with others. Our journey (IN) is the joining together of a body, connected to a head, which is Christ. I can only be fully me with you. I need to be rooted with you. We need to be rooted together.

This truth is seen even in the life of trees. Scientists like Dr. Nalini Nadkarni explain how seemingly dead tree stumps find a way to produce new living tissue. The secret is in the roots:

> Down there, hidden under the surface, lies a vast network of tree roots. These networks are often called neighborhoods. Tree roots can leak out sugars and other compounds into the soil. Those sugars are then sucked up by neighboring roots.
>
> Tree roots can also share nutrients with far-away neighbors by transporting them across thin threads of fungi. These threads spread through the soil like giant underground spider webs. They penetrate the roots of neighboring trees, creating pathways that exchange hormones and other material.

Beyond this, Dr. Nadkarni points to something called root grafting.

> It happens when tree roots rub against each other and physically fuse together. When this occurs, neighboring trees—even different species—share one big circulatory system. It's like connecting blood vessels of two different people. One tree gives the other tree a permanent transfusion.[3]

The connection of root systems is life and healing. It's true for trees. It's true for us, too. Individuals living rooted together, grafted together, rubbing up against each other, sharing resources, giving life. This union is essential. We will not survive alone. We simply won't make it. Frodo had a fellowship. So did Jesus. We are meant to live connected. This is not a solo gig.

> You can trust us to stick to you through thick and thin—
> to the bitter end. And you can trust us to keep any secret of
> yours—closer than you yourself keep it. But you cannot trust
> us to let you face trouble alone, and go off without a word. We
> are your friends, Frodo. Anyway: there it is. We know most
> of what Gandalf has told you. We know a good deal about the
> ring. We are horribly afraid—but we are coming with you; or
> following you like hounds.[4]

I need the voices of others speaking into my life, following me like hounds, protecting, defending, encouraging, adventuring, celebrating. Together we become something vibrant and alive and transformative. All by myself, it can get pretty weird. Without this kind of connection, I think I might spend most of my days in bed with a bag of chocolate sandwich cookies.

This is the beauty of a fellowship. A cohort. A body. People around us who can do what we can't do, what we're not made to do. A hand needs a foot. An arm needs a leg. Each part is uniquely crafted to fit together, to work together. So it is with us as we live in God. "Just as a body, though one, has many parts, but all its many parts form one body, so it is with Christ."[5]

God is making two (or more) one all the time. His purpose has always been peace. The death of our hostility toward one another. He tears down the dividing walls between Jew and Greek, male and female, slave and free. He makes us one new humanity.

BELONGING

This new humanity is captured in the African value and practice of *ubuntu*, derived from a Nguni word meaning "the quality of being human." According to sociolinguist Buntu Mfenyana, it "runs through the veins of all Africans, is embodied in the oft-repeated *Ubuntu ngumtu ngabanye abantu* ('A person is a person through other people')."[6] In a world where we are increasingly divided by color and nationality and sexuality and politics and poverty, *ubuntu* shows us the way to live in our shared humanity, honoring, affirming, belonging.

"A person with ubuntu," writes Desmond Tutu, "is open and available to others, affirming of others, does not feel threatened that others are able and good, for he or she has a proper self-assurance that comes from knowing that he or she belongs in a greater whole and is diminished when others are humiliated or diminished, when others are tortured or oppressed."[7]

This *ubuntu* sense that we belong to a greater whole—this is the essence of (IN). In his letter to the Roman church, the apostle Paul writes, "For just as each of us has one body with many members, and these members do not all have the same function, so in Christ we, though many, form one body, and each member belongs to all the others."[8]

I'm not really a fan of this belonging thing. I mean, I like the idea of being a part of something, part of the fellowship for sure. But I also like my distance, my rights, my ability to choose what I want when I want it. And belonging, as in actually belonging to one another, pretty much annihilates all that. There's no room for special privilege here, and as an "enneagram 4" I like special a lot. Belonging requires submission, all the parts laying aside their individual rights to be right, so the body can move and live and thrive.

Submission. Also a word I'm not fond of. Because it's often abused and misused, particularly when it's directed at women. But the invitation to submission is relational, not hierarchical. Submission is not permission for a top-down power play. It does not place one above the other. It places us side by side, inviting us to make room for one another. Submission is the choice love makes to value the other, to set aside our differences and offenses, to honor, to prefer.

"Submit to one another out of reverence for Christ."[9] This directive from Paul follows the prayer of Ephesians 3, that we would know the expanse of God's love. And it follows his words in Ephesians 4: "Make every effort to keep the unity of the Spirit through the bond of peace. There is one body and one Spirit, just as you were called to one hope when you were called; one Lord, one faith, one baptism; one God and Father of all, who is over all and through all and in all."[10] This mutual submission assumes a knowing of love and oneness. Only from this place can we choose the other over self. Here, in submission, the dying of self leads to the resurrection of the body. In the words of Martin Luther King:

> And whatever affects one directly affects all indirectly. For some strange reason, I can never be what I ought to be until you are what you ought to be. And you can never be what you ought to be until I am what I ought to be. This is the way God's universe is made; this is the way it is structured.[11]

TEACH US TO PRAY

I'm beginning to think that it's not fully possible to embody Jesus individually. That we can only fully embody Jesus corporately. As a body of believers. A fellowship. Maybe this is why Jesus teaches the disciples to pray in the plural. Our Father. Give us. Lead us. Deliver us. There's nothing individual or singular here. His prayer is undivided. This is how Jesus teaches us to pray. And this is how his prayer is answered. In the words of Thomas Merton:

> After all, transformation into Christ is not just an individual affair: there is only one Christ, not many. He is not

divided. And for me to become Christ is to enter into the Life of the Whole Christ, the Mystical Body made up of the Head and its members, Christ and all who are incorporated in Him by His Spirit.

Christ forms Himself by grace and faith in the souls of all who love Him, and at the same time He draws them all together in Himself to make them One in Him. . . . And the Holy Ghost, Who is the life of this One Body dwells in the whole Body and in every one of the members so that the whole Christ is Christ and each individual is Christ.[12]

After Jesus talks about abiding and pruning and the promise of the coming of Holy Spirit—the last things he shares with his friends before his death—he prays. This is his last prayer on Earth. And it's all about (IN). Our oneness is the point.

I pray also for those who will believe in me through their message, that all of them may be one, Father, just as you are in me and I am in you. May they also be in us so that the world may believe that you have sent me. I have given them the glory that you gave me, that they may be one as we are one—I in them and you in me—so that they may be brought to complete unity. Then the world will know that you sent me and have loved them even as you have loved me.[13]

Jesus prays this amazing, confounding prayer. A seemingly unanswerable prayer that communicates the deepest intention of his life and death and resurrection. He prays that we would be one with him as he is one with the Father, that we would be one with each other. In a world increasingly fragmented, fearful, and partisan, the answer to this prayer seems impossible. But the truth is, God has already made the way, and the way is (IN). In Jesus, he invites us to live connected with God, with ourselves and with others in truth and in grace, rooted and grounded in love.

Jesus, in essence, prays that we would fulfill the greatest command-ment: that we would love God and love our neighbors as ourselves. And we are the answer to that prayer, as we submit to one another in love.

LISTENING TO HEAL THE BODY

Healing this mystical body, becoming fully human together and embodying Jesus on the planet, loving our neighbor, living undi-vided—it all begins with connection. Sitting together, face to face, hearing one another's stories. Looking into one another's eyes and finding ourselves. Allowing our lives to touch, to rub up against each other. Maybe at the most basic level, all this begins with listening. Simply being present with others. Submitting and setting aside my need to be heard, to advise, to assert my opinion, to be right, to be the center. Listening—really listening to the heart, simply to under-stand—this is where healing begins.

Theologian Dietrich Bonhoeffer, author of the classic *The Cost of Discipleship*, wrote about the importance of listening:

> There is a kind of listening with half an ear that pre-sumes already to know what the other person has to say. It is an impatient, inattentive listening, that despises the brother and is only waiting for a chance to speak and thus get rid of the other person. This is no fulfillment of our obligation, and it is certain that here too our attitude toward our brother only reflects our relationship to God. It is little wonder that we are no longer capable of the greatest service of listening that God has committed to us, that of hear-ing our brother's confession, if we refuse to give ear to our brother on lesser subjects. Secular education today is aware that often a person can be helped merely by having someone

who will listen to him seriously, and upon this insight it has constructed its own soul therapy, which has attracted great numbers of people, including Christians. But Christians have forgotten that the ministry of listening has been committed to them by Him who is Himself the great listener and whose work they should share. We should listen with the ears of God that we may speak the Word of God.[14]

This kind of listening is experienced as love. In the words of Mr. Rogers, "Listening is where love begins: listening to ourselves and then to our neighbors."[15]

When my daughter is sharing something in her life that's painful or isn't going well, maybe a relationship that's challenging, my first instinct always is to advise—to share all my knowing, help set things right, make the pain stop. (I have the very best intentions; really, I do.) And when I do this (which is almost always), it never goes well. I should know better by now, right? But I can't seem to help myself. Until she looks at me and says, with a definite edge to her voice, "You're not listening." Right. OK, listening expert, just listen.

And in a moment, the whole dynamic changes. She feels heard. She feels understood. She feels loved. And in this connected place, she finds a way through that's better than anything I had to offer. It's beautiful. And humbling. And so, so good.

While there's never a magic formula in life, for listening . . . there kind of is. Reflective listening combines the thought the person is sharing with the emotion that goes with it, and offers these back with a tentative opening: "It sounds like you're worried about meeting the deadline for your project." "It seems like you're angry with your mom because she's critical." You get the idea.

And here's the best news: You don't even have to get these right. You can miss the thought or emotion or both, and it still works. Because in listening and offering your statements tentatively, you are opening safe space to react and refine. "No, I'm not angry at my mom. I'm sad because I'd really like to have a better relationship with her." Score. You've created space for them to express and explore and continue the conversation. And in this space, the healing power of connection happens.

Brené Brown writes, "If we can share our story with someone who responds with empathy and understanding, shame can't survive."[16] Shame is the sense that I am wrong, that there is something wrong with me at the very core. Empathy takes "wrong" out of the equation. When I listen and respond with empathy, I communicate that I can identify with and understand your emotions and perspectives. You are not alone in your experience. Empathy levels the playing field. It submits to the other, and it places us side by side in our shared human experience. From Henri Nouwen:

> To listen is very hard, because it asks of us so much interior stability that we no longer need to prove ourselves by speeches, arguments, statements, or declarations. True listeners no longer have an inner need to make their presence known. They are free to receive, to welcome, to accept.
>
> Listening is much more than allowing another to talk while waiting for a chance to respond. Listening is paying full attention to others and welcoming them into our very beings. The beauty of listening is that, those who are listened to start feeling accepted, start taking their words more seriously and discovering their own true selves.
>
> Listening is a form of spiritual hospitality by which you invite strangers to become friends, to get to know their inner selves more fully, and even to dare to be silent with you.[17]

HEALING THE BODY

Life, healing, and our ultimate becoming happen only in union. Only as we journey (IN) together. As we do the work of honoring the sacred and holy in each of us, as we lean in close enough to hear the heartbeat of Jesus in one another, as we practice *ubuntu*, the body begins to heal. Rooted together, sharing nutrients, rubbing up against one another, we find what we need to heal the broken body of Jesus.

This healing, the removing of the things that divide us, can only happen in safe, listening, honoring spaces. Spaces of belonging. Where it's OK to be honest and real and in process. To bring our pain and shame and disappointments into the light together. Listening and praying and breaking bread together, submitting our lives to one another, we find the way to union.

In Christ, we are body together. Jesus enfleshed. His hands, feet, eyes, ears, and heart walking around the planet, doing what he did. Rescuing. Saving. Healing. And inviting everyone to the party. I cannot be fully me without you. I am yours. You are mine. We are messy and marvelous. We are brave and bruised and beautiful. We are Christ's. We are one. And when people find a place like this, there will be a line out the door.

DEEPER (IN)

Living Undivided

Set aside some time in a quiet space where you won't be disturbed. Sit silently for a few moments. Recognize Holy Spirit's presence with you and in you. Breathe. Release distractions as they come.

As you feel centered, read this prayer from Jesus slowly three times: "I pray also for those who will believe in me through their message, that all of them may be one, Father, just as you are in me and I am in you. May they also be in us so that the world may believe that you have sent me."

Ask Holy Spirit how he's inviting you to live in a more unified way with others. How are your beliefs about others distorted? What attitudes or judgments divide you from others? Where do these beliefs, attitudes, judgments come from? Listen.

How does God want to restore connection and bring healing today? Do you feel prompted to turn from particular attitudes or judgments? To ask for forgiveness from him or from someone you've wronged? To forgive someone who's hurt you? Respond as you feel led.

Consider if there's someone you might want to reach out to—perhaps to repair broken relationship, or to initiate relationship with someone who's different from you. Spend time with that person listening to their story.

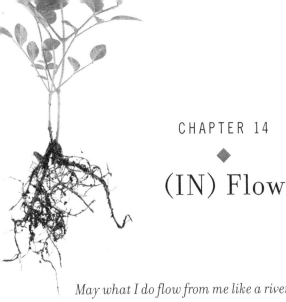

CHAPTER 14

◆

(IN) Flow

May what I do flow from me like a river, no forcing and
no holding back, the way it is with children.
—RAINER MARIA RILKE[1]

I WAS DRIVING AND listening to Judith MacNutt talk about healing. A friend was just back from attending the second level of the School of Healing Prayer offered by Judith and her husband Francis; and she was sharing all the training materials with me. My husband and I were attending a small Bible church at the time, and I'd been asked to start a prayer ministry there. I'd been noticing that God was drawing several people passionate about healing prayer to this little church, and I was wondering if God was up to something.

In the middle of a sentence about something unrelated, Judith mentioned their healing rooms. "Healing rooms . . . healing rooms . . . healing rooms." The words echoed around the car, seemingly louder and louder. The air felt thick with presence. And I saw an image in my mind of a funnel. Within the funnel, God was connecting different modalities of healing from around the city so people could find the resources and professionals they needed. People would emerge from the funnel ready to give away what they'd received.

Did I mention I was driving? It seemed like questionable timing to me, all that distraction while I was on the road. The words and thickness and image lasted just a few moments. But I knew this was an invitation. And I've learned on this journey, when God has an idea, it's best to just say yes. "God, I have no idea what you mean by healing rooms. But if you want to do this, I'm in. I have no idea how to do this, so you go, you make the way, and I'll follow." End of prayer.

A few days later, I was meeting with Dave Ping, Director of Equipping Ministries International (EMI). I'd been helping Dave develop some new curriculum on how we discover and live in our heart's desires. We'd talked before about my passion for prayer and healing, so I was sharing with him what had happened in the car. Healing rooms and all that.

Dave's eyes got big. "Susan, God's been telling us for a year to get back to our roots in healing. We've been praying, asking him to bring the person to do it. If you think it's you, then would you consider doing it here, with us?" God was already on the move, with something in mind. And I was being invited to step into the flow.

Nearly thirty years prior, Dr. Gary Sweeten had started a ministry at College Hill Presbyterian Church. He'd developed courses in listening, renewing the mind, and more. And teams were trained to meet with people to listen and pray with them for healing. Holy Spirit was moving in renewal in the church, and people's lives were being transformed. EMI grew from this ministry, equipping people around the world in these skills. Over the years, the emphasis had moved from hands-on healing to equipping. God was calling them back to their roots.

Within a week, I joined EMI. I now had infrastructure and the ability to raise funds for this new work. God was beginning to fill in the picture for me, showing me more of what he had in mind. The church gave us a room to use, our first healing room. And three of us began to meet with people by appointment for listening and healing prayer. Word spread, and emails started coming from people around the city who also had vision for this kind of work. God was reconnecting relationships formed over decades in the city. I was amazed. And humbled. I'd been invited into something already happening, a river already flowing—and I was being carried in the current.

Since that time, Roots&Branches has grown to become its own 501(c)(3) with a reach across our city and beyond. And I've grown, too, through challenges and resistance and deep disappointments. Passion, gifts, experiences, learnings developing in me for decades are now being poured out.

Our teams have met with hundreds of people, and we've equipped hundreds more in listening and healing prayer. We have the honor of sitting with people, creating safe sacred space where they can share their stories. As we help them connect with Jesus, listening to Holy Spirit, we witness the most amazing encounters. Really, it takes my breath away. God comes to meet each one personally, uniquely, right in the middle of their pain. He comes to restore, to heal, to redeem. And we get front row seats to grace. This is better than anything I could have asked or imagined. It's the adventure of a lifetime.

FLOW

Jesus lived in flow. So did his friends, aka disciples. With a simple invitation, "Follow me," men and women left behind everything to go on the road with Jesus. No persuasive sales pitch here—just an invitation to an adventure as wandering ragamuffins, keeping company with God himself. They had no idea what they were saying "yes" to. But somehow they recognized God was on the move. Something was afoot, and they gave everything, literally, to be a part of it.

This flow is inherently relational. It occurs within the nature of God. Father, Son, Spirit, three in one, giving and receiving. Jesus in us. Spirit in us. You and me in God. This union isn't static. It's dynamic, moving, always initiating and sustaining connection. All the time. We are invited to live and move and breathe (IN) this flow.

"I only do what I see my Father doing."[2] From this connection with Father, Jesus acted. He blessed the loaves and fishes knowing his Father

was multiplying. He touched the lepers knowing his Father was healing. He spoke knowing his Father was calming the storm or raising the
dead. We are invited to live in this same flow. Abiding in the vine, we
become part of the flow—living water moving from roots to fruit.

"Be fruitful and multiply." From the garden forward, this has
been the word of God to us. This fruit multiplies only through the
life-giving, life-sustaining flow of Spirit. Fruitfulness requires flow.

Jesus says it another way. Remember Chapter 2? It all comes back
to abiding. We are made to bear fruit, and this fruit is love. Love in,
love out. This is prayer. This is joy. This is life-flowing connection to
the fullest.

> This is to my Father's glory, that you bear much fruit,
> showing yourselves to be my disciples.
>
> As the Father has loved me, so have I loved you. Now
> remain in my love. If you keep my commands, you will
> remain in my love, just as I have kept my Father's com-
> mands and remain in his love. I have told you this so that
> my joy may be in you and that your joy may be complete.[3]

Remaining in this love sustains the flow that leads to fruitfulness. We do not produce fruit. We yield fruit. All that's needed is
supplied to us from the vine. Connected to the vine, we receive all
we need. Fruit is the natural byproduct of connection, of flow. A tree
does not yield a pear because it tries really hard. It is in the nature
of a pear tree to yield pears. It is in our nature, as bearers of the living God, to yield life. Yielding fruit, we become trees of life, offering
soul sustenance to those around us. Andrew Murray writes,

> If Christ, the Heavenly Vine, has taken the believer as
> a branch, then He has pledged himself, in the very nature
> of things, to supply the sap, spirit, and nourishment to

make it bear fruit. The soul need to concern itself with one thing—to abide closely, fully, and entirely to Him. Christ will give the fruit. He works all that is needed to make the believer a blessing.[4]

Connected in the relational, creative flow of Spirit, we become blessing. Life in. Life out. And the out is really the point. Because out is the place of joy. As we love one another, we experience his joy in us, and this joy is made complete, mature, full in us. This is not a giddy happiness that depends on circumstances. But a deep, sustaining joy that remains as we remain (IN) the flow.

FRUIT THAT LASTS

The fruit we bear comes in different shapes and sizes. It comes in different seasons, in different ways at different times. My fruit often comes in the shape of healing. Sometimes it looks like kindness or leadership or administration. Your fruit will show the shape of the gifts given and the character formed in you over time. Perhaps hospitality or mercy or prophecy or service. One shape isn't better than any other. One size isn't better than any other. One season isn't better than any other. It all feeds people hungry for a taste of God.

We tend to value bigger and faster. We want to be used by God in ways that feel important. But God isn't interested in pop-up fruit stands and overnight flashy fruit success. And he isn't a user, a power-wielding vineyard owner using us to produce. He's after friendship and fruit that lasts.

My command is this: Love each other as I have loved you. Greater love has no one than this: to lay down one's life for one's friends. You are my friends if you do what I command. I no longer call you servants, because a servant does not know his master's business. Instead, I have called you friends, for everything that I learned from my Father I have made known to you. You did not choose me, but I chose you and appointed you so that you might go and bear fruit—fruit that will last—and so that whatever you ask in my name the Father will give you. This is my command: Love each other.[5]

We are appointed to bear fruit. It's what we're made for. And it comes at a cost. It comes with the emptying of self. Removing the things in our root systems that block and hinder the flow of love. Becoming vulnerable. Laying down our lives for others. Following the way of humility. Going lower, laying aside privilege and power. With Jesus, the lowest place becomes the highest place, the place of resurrection, new life. Our fruitfulness requires this same yielding. From Henri Nouwen:

> The question is: "Are you going to bear fruit?" And the amazing thing is that our fruitfulness comes out of our vulnerability, not out of our power. Actually, it comes out of our powerlessness. If the ground wants to be fruitful, you have to break it open a bit. The hard ground cannot bear fruit; it has to be raked open. . . . Precisely where we are weakest and often most broken and most needy, precisely there can be the ground of our fruitfulness.[6]

Fruitfulness—the kind of fruit that lasts—doesn't depend on our ability, our strength, our gifting or our trying harder. It depends on our yielding and abiding. It depends on our yes to less. And somehow, in this place of less, space is opened within to hold more, to hold the fullness of joy that is Christ.

NOTICING

Jesus was just passing through, on his way to the next town.[7] Jericho wasn't his destination. Jericho wasn't the point that day. But then

Jesus, just having a day, looks up and notices a particular guy in a particular tree. Zacchaeus had climbed up, perhaps with others, to catch a glimpse of Jesus. The crowd, all eager to be near Jesus, made it impossible for Zacchaeus to see. He was, apparently, on the shorter side. So this rich man, a wealthy tax collector and well-known "sinner," climbed.

"Zacchaeus, come down immediately. I must stay at your house today." And with that, plans changed. Jesus invites himself over for a dinner party, and Zacchaeus is changed. While others grumble, ticked off because Jesus has noticed and chosen this sinner, Zacchaeus pledges publicly to give half of what he has to the poor and to pay back those he's cheated four times over. Zacchaeus says one big yes to saving grace, and he jumps with both feet into the flow of God. Jesus says this is why he came, to seek and to save. This is why he stops on his way somewhere else—because he notices a man in a tree, and he knows in his knower that his Father is up to something.

Jesus, moved by compassion, stopped for people along the way all the time as he became aware his Father was working. We are invited to live in this same flow every day as we have ears to hear, eyes to see, and a yes to yield. This kind of flow doesn't always feel flowy, natural, or easy. Most days don't feel flowy to me at all. Much of most days I'm working my agenda, on my way somewhere. Laundry, dinner, meetings, prayer sessions, momming, shopping—there's a lot going on. It all feels super-important, and much of it is. But if I'm watching, noticing, aware, and willing to suspend my plans for a hot minute, I may just get to be a part of something the Father is doing. He is always inviting. And we get to invite, too. Noticing the needs around us, watching for ways to bring love to the party, we join Jesus in his healing, restoring, making-all-things-new revolution. Bob Goff writes,

Every day God invites us on the same kind of adventure.
It's not a trip where He sends us a rigid itinerary, He simply

invites us. God asks what it is He's made us to love, what it is that captures our attention, what feeds that deep indescribable need of our souls to experience the richness of the world He made. And then, leaning over us, He whispers, "Let's go do that together."[8]

In the late 1980s my search for people who were doing the stuff I saw Jesus doing led me to Vineyard Community Church in Cincinnati, Ohio. In the 1990s the pastor, Steve Sjogren, began a local movement that has gone global. This movement, known as servant evangelism, is all about kindness with no strings attached. Inspired by Mother Teresa who said, "Not all of us can do great things. But we can do small things with great love," Steve led us in simple, small acts of kindness. Giving away bottled water on hot days, washing cars for free, scrubbing toilets in restaurants and bars, wrapping Christmas gifts for free at a local mall, and more. Sometimes we'd get to pray with people. Sometimes we simply got to be Jesus present with people for a moment. Showing them what God's love is like. Free. No strings attached. This is some of the best fun I've had in my life, learning to watch for creative opportunities to love and serve.

Some time ago, waiting in line to pay for my groceries, I had one of these noticing moments. I felt the familiar nudge as I looked at the cashier. "Pray for her." Seriously, God? There are people in line behind me. This really doesn't seem like a good time. I had lots of reasons for no. But the nudge kept coming.

As she checked out my items, I asked how she was doing. Instead of responding with the usual, "Fine," she started to tell me her story. She was having back issues and was in a lot of pain. I listened. Empathized. Then I dove in the flow. I looked her in the eyes and spoke a blessing over her and her back, and asked God to take the pain away. It was a few seconds. And in just a few seconds her entire countenance changed. She immediately looked lighter. She thanked me with a very big smile on her face and said she was already feeling a little better. She felt blessed, but I think I got the bigger blessing. There's so much joy in the overflow. And I almost missed it.

AN INVITATION TO ADVENTURE

God is inviting us to adventure with him all the time. In big and small ways, every day, he invites us to join him in what he's doing. To jump in the river of grace and go with the flow. We are made for good works, as the apostle Paul wrote in his letter to the Ephesians, "We are what [God] has made us, created in Christ Jesus for good works which God prepared beforehand to be our way of life."[9] With the help of theologian N. T. Wright, we find the invitation:

> Now you may well feel that phrase "good works" is a bit ho-hum, a bit "oh dear, here we go, we've got to behave ourselves" and all that sort of thing. But it's not like that at all. The word in the Greek for "what He has made us" means we are God's poem; we are God's artwork. God has given us many gifts. The good works that we are to do are not simply referring to moral behavior. God wants us to be fruitful. God wants us to be experimental. God wants us to be innovative. . . . We are God's work of art, created in Christ Jesus to do good works. And it's not that we necessarily make His world a glorious place as much as we remind the world that it is a glorious place.[10]

We are invited to co-create with God in ways that are unique to each of us, fitted to the way we're made. Every day we are invited to experiment, to love in creative ways, to create in loving ways, all to remind the people around us that they're carrying glory. This is Christ in us, setting out to love the world back into wholeness. To restore. To encourage. To bless.

Our neighbors are all around us. They are like us and so very different from us. And our call to love them as we love ourselves is a call to a radical, creative revolution of kindness. Because love acts. Or in Bob Goff's words, "Love does." Our contemplation and prayer must always have an outward, social expression. It can only exist in flow. Life in. Life out. Love in. Love out. Without this flow, we become stagnant and stale. In flow, we thrive.

If life feels stagnant and stale, if your heart has gone numb, if disappointments have dulled your desire, will you dare to listen within again? Invite God to meet you in your story. To remind you who you really are. To breathe life within and fan the creative spark. He's inviting you to dream with him, to create with him, to join with him in what he's doing on the earth today. He's already prepared the way. And he's waiting for your yes.

This is the end game. The point of it all. Partnering with God to restore blessing, to restore creation, not only in the future, but in the now. You're invited to this partnership, this friendship with God and others. Living connected, abiding in flow, bringing the fruit that feeds the earth.

This flow begins and ends in a garden. With a tree that bears the fruit of life. United in the creative flow of life and love to the earth—feeding the hungry, caring for the poor, freeing the prisoners, healing the sick—we become part of the river that feeds the trees, that produces the fruit, that heals the nations.

> Then the angel showed me the river of the water of life, as clear as crystal, flowing from the throne of God and of the Lamb down the middle of the great street of the city. On each side of the river stood the tree of life, bearing twelve crops of fruit, yielding its fruit every month. And the leaves of the tree are for the healing of the nations.[11]

DEEPER (IN)

Here are two ways you can dive into the flow. Pick the one that resonates the most with you right now. Or do both if you like. It's your adventure. You get to choose.

Today's Adventure

While you're out and about today or tomorrow, ask God to help you notice what he's doing. Then watch to see if someone is highlighted to you. Who do you notice? What nudge do you feel from God? Maybe it's simply to smile and be present to them. To pray silently for them. Maybe it's to do something more. Take the risk and dive in.

Afterward, take a few minutes to write about the experience. How did it feel? If it feels hard to move out of your comfort zone and take the risk, remember, all is grace. All is flow. What would it look like for you to experience more flow in your life? Ask God to make you more sensitive to what he's doing around you as you move through life. If you're feeling stagnant or disconnected, ask him what's clogging up the flow.

The Next Big Adventure

You are shaped for something, a something only you can bring. A type of fruit only you can yield. And we need your something. Really we do. As you live (IN), your desires will lead you there. The desires at the core, placed there by God. These, together with your gifts and talents and experiences and the compassion you feel, all point you toward your adventure.

For me, healing was a part of me from day one with Jesus. But it's also evident again and again in my story. The stories in my life that resonate, the times I've felt most alive, almost all have the same theme. Healing. Restoration. Renewal. As you listen to your life with God, what moments have felt most alive to you? Do you see themes there, something they have in common?

Set some time aside in a quiet place. (You know the drill.) Maybe it's time to pull out the big guns and schedule a silent retreat. A day or two or more away for listening prayer and reflection. If this isn't possible for you right now, that's OK. Take some smaller chunks of time for listening.

Ask the Lord what he's inviting you to in this season of your life. Is there a new adventure he's calling you to? Listen to God. Listen to your life. You might look again at the life map you created in Chapter 10. What moments have felt most alive to you? What themes do you see across the meaningful moments of your life? What are the desires of your heart that just don't go away over time? Where do your gifts and talents and passions meet? Is there something here for you to notice?

If something rises to the top, something he's inviting to, what's your response? You might write about how this feels to you. When you're ready to give your yes, find a river stone, a smooth one. (You can get them at craft stores or perhaps in your back yard.) With a black Sharpie, write your YES on the stone to signify you're diving into the river. Keep your YES stone in a prominent place as a stone of remembrance.

We awaken in Christ's body,
As Christ awakens our bodies
There I look down and my poor hand is Christ,
He enters my foot and is infinitely me.
I move my hand and wonderfully
My hand becomes Christ,
Becomes all of Him.
I move my foot and at once
He appears in a flash of lightning.
Do my words seem blasphemous to you?
—Then open your heart to Him.
And let yourself receive the one
Who is opening to you so deeply.
For if we genuinely love Him,
We wake up inside Christ's body
Where all our body all over,
Every most hidden part of it,
Is realized in joy as Him,
And He makes us utterly real.
And everything that is hurt, everything
That seemed to us dark, harsh, shameful,
maimed, ugly, irreparably damaged
Is in Him transformed.
And in Him, recognized as whole, as lovely,
And radiant in His light,
We awaken as the beloved
In every last part of our body.

—Symeon the New Theologian[12]

CREATING
A ROOTED
COMMUNITY

A ROOTED LIFE IS lived in community, and this rooted journey is best taken with a tribe, large or small. Your tribe might be a few good friends, a small group, a church. People who will encourage you in your becoming. People who will partner in creating safe, healing spaces for connection with God and with one another.

What are the hallmarks of a rooted community?

Noise-free. Rooted communities are full of listening people. People who value listening to God and listening to one another. Who make silence safe and cultivate contemplative spaces for prayerful connection.

Shame-free. Rooted communities are full of safe people. People who encourage, cheer, and challenge. Who do not judge. Who accept you, see the best, offer grace, and call you in love into your true self.

Formula-free. Rooted communities are full of people who embrace process. People who do not offer easy answers or steps to growth and freedom. Who are on a lifelong journey of healing and becoming as they live by Spirit and follow Jesus together.

Our team at Roots&Branches Network brings messages, courses, and workshops to help you grow a more rooted life and community. Find out more at susancarson.net, or at rootsandbranchesnetwork.com.

ENDNOTES

INTRODUCTION

1 Henri Nouwen, *The Inner Voice of Love: A Journey Through Anguish to Freedom* (New York: Random House, 1996), 94.

2 Thomas Merton, *New Seeds of Contemplation* (New York: New Directions, 1961), 75.

3 J. R. R. Tolkien, *The Fellowship of the Ring* (New York: Houghton Mifflin, 1965), 325.

OPENER PAGE

1 Peter Wohlleben, *The Hidden Life of Trees: What They Feel, How They Communicate* (Munich: Random House, 2015), 81.

CHAPTER ONE

1 Victor Hugo, *The Hunchback of Notre Dame* (New York: Macmillan Collector's Library, 2004), 478.

2 Genesis 3:10.

3 Ephesians 3:16–19.

4 Brené Brown, *The Gifts of Imperfection* (Center City, MN: Hazelden Publishing, 2010), 19.

5 Merton, *New Seeds of Contemplation*, 14.

6 Matthew 13:3–9.

7 Revelation 22:1–2.

CHAPTER TWO

1 Paulo Coelho, *The Alchemist* (New York: HarperOne, 1993), 147.

2 John 15:1–5.

3 John 15:9–17.

4 John 10:30.

5 John 14:15–21.

6 Andrew Murray, *Abiding in Christ* (Minneapolis: Bethany House, 2003), 38.

7 Leanne Payne, *Real Presence* (Grand Rapids, MI: Hamewith Books, 1995), 31.

8 Acts 17:28.

9 Romans 8:38–39.

10 Richard Rohr, "Life as Participation: In Christ," Richard Rohr's Daily Meditation, September 18, 2014, https://mye-mail.constantcontact.com/Richard-Rohr-s-Meditation--In-Christ.html?soid=1103098668616&aid=y3Sik2PEOdo.

11 James Bryan Smith, "The Highest Form of Prayer," in *Devotional Classics*, eds. Richard Foster and James Bryan Smith (San Francisco: HarperCollins, 2005), 77.

12 Philippians 3:9.

13 Romans 7:15.

14 Murray, *Abiding in Christ*, 26.

15 "Lorica of St. Patrick," EWTN Global Catholic Network, https://www.ewtn.com/devotionals/prayers/patrick.htm.

16 John Eldredge, "Daily Prayer," Ransomed Heart Ministries, https://www.ransomedheart.com/prayer/daily-prayer.

17 Henri Nouwen, *You Are the Beloved: Daily Meditations for Spiritual Living* (New York: Convergent, 2017), 165.

CHAPTER THREE

1 Annie Dillard, *Teaching a Stone to Talk: Expeditions and Encounters* (New York: HarperCollins, 1982), 85.

2 John 1:18.

3 1 John 1:1.

4 Matthew 3:17.

5 John 5:19–20.

6 Mother Teresa, *In the Heart of the World: Thoughts, Stories and Prayers* (Novato, CA: New World Library, 1995), 19.

7 Matthew 17:1–13.

8 John 16:12–15.

9 John 10:3–5, 27.

10 Romans 10:17 ESV.

11 Quoted in Foster and Smith, *Devotional Classics*, 81.

12 This story appears in 1 Samuel 3.

13 Numbers 22:21–35.

14 A. W. Tozer, "Hearing God's Voice," The Alliance Tozer Devotional, https://www.cmalliance.org/devotions/tozer?id=1096.

15 This story appears in John 4.

16 Foster, *Prayer*, 149–150.

CHAPTER FOUR

1 George MacDonald, *The Marquis of Lossie*, Project Gutenberg, http://www.gutenberg.org/files/7174/7174-h/7174-h.htm.

2 A. W. Tozer, *The Knowledge of the Holy* (New York: HarperCollins, 1978), 1.

3 John 14:9.

4 Brennan Manning, *Ruthless Trust: The Ragamuffin's Path to God* (New York: HarperCollins, 2000), 88.

5 Jesus told this story, often known as the story of the prodigal son, in Luke 15:11–32.

6 Psalm 22:1–11.

7 Psalm 22:14.

8 Psalm 22:22–24.

9 1 John 4:16.

10 Jeremiah 17:7–8.

CHAPTER FIVE

1   Quoted in Anne Lamott, "Anne Lamott Shares All That She Knows," *Salon*, April 10, 2015, https://www.salon.com/2015/04/10/anne_lamott_shares_all_that_she_knows_everyone_is_screwed_up_broken_clingy_and_scared.

2   Quoted in John Ortberg, "Ruthlessly Eliminate Hurry," *Christianity Today* Pastors, July 2002, https://www.christianitytoday.com/pastors/2002/july-online-only/cln20704.html.

3   Isaiah 30:15.

4   Richard Rohr, "Wholeness: Being in God," Richard Rohr's Daily Meditation, November 13, 2014.

5   Quoted in Foster and Smith, *Devotional Classics*, 82.

6   Shauna Niequist, *Present over Perfect* (Grand Rapids, MI: Zondervan, 2016), 93.

7   Psalm 46:10.

8   Matthew 11:28–30.

9   Luke 4:14 MSG.

10 Mark 1:35 RSV.

11 Foster, *Prayer*, 101.

12 Quoted in Richard J. Foster, *Celebration of Discipline: The Path to Spiritual Growth* (San Francisco: HarperCollins, 1984), 96.

13 Julian of Norwich, *Julian of Norwich: Showings*, trans. Edmund Colledge and James Walsh (Mahwah, NJ: Paulist Press, 1977), 254.

14 Psalm 34:8.

15 Quoted in James W. Goll, *The Lost Art of Practicing His Presence* (Shippensburg, PA: Destiny Image Publishers, 2005), 238.

16 Foster, *Celebration of Discipline*, 96–97.

17 Quoted in Foster and Smith, *Devotional Classics*, 359.

CHAPTER SIX

1 Oscar Wilde, "*De Profundis*," The Literature Network, http://www.online-literature.com/wilde/1306.

2 Henri Nouwen, "Baptism and Eucharist," Henri Nouwen's Bread for the Journey, September 24, Henri Nouwen Society, https://henrinouwen.org/meditation/baptism-and-eucharist.

3 This story appears in Exodus 16.

4 John 6:48–50, 56–57.

5 Luke 22:19–20.

6 Foster, *Prayer*, 112.

7 Richard Rohr, "Eucharist: Jesus in Me and Me in Jesus," Richard Rohr's Daily Meditation, September 23, 2014, https://myemail.constantcontact.com/Richard-Rohr-s-Meditation--Jesus-in-Me-and-Me-in-Jesus.html?soid=1103098668616&aid=_BBR9LP2hvY.

8 Matthew 3:16–17.

9 Matthew 4:4.

10 John 1:1–5.

11 John 15:3–4.

12 Neiquist, *Present over Perfect*, 82.

13 Payne, *Real Presence*, 35.

14 1 Corinthians 11:24–26.

15 Matthew 6:9–13.

CHAPTER SEVEN

1 Frances Chan, *Forgotten God: Reversing Our Tragic Neglect of the Holy Spirit* (Colorado Springs: David C. Cook, 2009), 142.

2 John 14:15–21.

3 John 14:23.

4 John 16:6–7, 12–15.

5 Quoted in Foster and Smith, *Devotional Classics*, 174.

6 Acts 2:1–4.

7 Ephesians 5:18–19.

8 Quoted in Foster and Smith, *Devotional Classics*, 143.

9 1 Corinthians 13:1–8.

10 N. T. Wright, *Simply Christian: Why Christianity Makes Sense* (New York: HarperCollins, 2006), 140.

11 Luke 4:17–19.

12 Murray, *Abide in Christ*, 30.

13 Ephesians 3:16–21.

14 Romans 15:13.

CHAPTER EIGHT

1 Elie Wiesel, "Oprah Talks to Elie Wiesel," *O Magazine*, November 2000, https://www.oprah.com/omagazine/oprah-interviews-elie-wiesel/2.

2 Luke 1:28.

3 John 1:14, 16–18.

4 Brennan Manning, *The Ragamuffin Gospel: Good News for the Bedraggled, Beat-Up, and Burnt Out* (Sisters, OR: Multnomah Books, 1990), 214.

5 Brené Brown, *Daring Greatly: How the Courage to Be Vulnerable Transforms the Way We Live, Love, Parent, and Lead* (New York: Gotham Books, 2012), 68–69.

6 Ephesians 2:4–9.

7 Matthew 21:13.

8 Richard Rohr, "Life as Participation: In Christ" Richard Rohr's Daily Meditation, September 18, 2014, https://myemail.constantcontact.com/Richard-Rohr-s-Meditation--In-Christ.html?soid=1103098668616&aid=y3Sik2PEOdo.

9 This story appears in Genesis 28.

10 Kathleen Norris, *Amazing Grace* (New York: Riverhead Books, 1998), 151.

11 2 Corinthians 12:8–10.

12 Scott Barry Kaufman, "Embrace the Uncool: Brené Brown on Overcoming Shame" *Heleo,* https://heleo.com/conversation-embrace-the-uncool-Brené-brown-on-overcoming-shame/12402.

13 Jacques Philippe, *Interior Freedom* (New York: Sceptre Publishers, 2007), 33.

14 Foster, *Prayer,* 27–29.

15 Psalm 85:10, KJV.

16 Rumi, *The Essential Rumi,* trans. Coleman Barks (New York: HarperCollins, 1995), 70.

17 Thomas Merton, "The Merton Prayer" Reflections, Yale University, https://reflections.yale.edu/article/seize-day-vocation-calling-work/merton-prayer.

CHAPTER NINE

1 Madeleine L'Engle, *A Circle of Quiet: The Crosswicks Journal* (San Francisco: Harper, 1972), Section 1.10.

2 John and Stasi Eldredge, *Captivating: Unveiling the Mystery of a Woman's Soul* (Nashville: Thomas Nelson, 2005), 56.

3 This story appears in Matthew 16:13–20.

4 This story appears in John 21.

5 Matthew 5:48.

6 Norris, *Amazing Grace,* 57.

7 1 John 4:16–19.

8 Eugene H. Peterson, *Run with the Horses: The Quest for Life at Its Best* (Downers Grove, IL: InterVarsity Press, 2009), 39–40.

9 Ephesians 4:20–24.

10 This story appears in John 11:1–43.

11 2 Corinthians 3:18.

12 Henri Nouwen, *You Are the Beloved: Daily Meditations for Spiritual Living* (New York: Convergent, 2017), 12.

13 Stasi Eldredge, *Becoming Myself: Embracing God's Dream of You* (Colorado Springs: David C. Cook, 2013), 23.

14 Psalm 139:13–16, 23–24.

15 Merton, *New Seeds of Contemplation*, 31.

16 This experience is adapted from Dr. Karl Lehman's Immanuel Approach, found at www.immanuelapproach.com.

CHAPTER TEN

1 Maya Angelou, *I Know Why the Caged Bird Sings* (New York: Random House, 1969), 74.

2 Brown, *The Gifts of Imperfection*, vii.

3 Quoted in Kara Kuruvilla, "Bono Has a Message for Young Christian Artists," Huffington Post, May 16, 2017, https://www.huffingtonpost.com/entry/bono-has-a-message-for-young-christian-artists_us_591b0b63e4b07d5f6ba62fc8.

4 Thomas Merton, *Thoughts in Solitude* (New York: Farrar, Status and Giroux, 1956), 33.

5 Psalm 118:1–4.

6 This story appears in Joshua 4–5.

7 This story appears in Exodus 33.

8 Ann Voskamp, *One Thousand Gifts* (Grand Rapids, MI: Zondervan, 2010), 156.

9 Brené Brown, "Own Our History. Change the Story," Brené Brown blog, June 18, 2015, https://Brenébrown.com/blog/2015/06/18/own-our-history-change-the-story/

10 Thomas Merton, *Seeds of Contemplation* (Norfolk, CT: New Directions, 1949), 14.

CHAPTER ELEVEN

1 Mary Oliver, *Thirst: Poems* (Boston: Beacon Press, 2006), 52.

2 This story appears in Genesis 32.

3 Hannah Hurnard, *Hinds' Feet on High Places* (Wheaton, IL: Tyndale House Publishers, 1977).

4 Voskamp, *One Thousand Gifts*, 84.

5 2 Corinthians 4:6–12, 16–18.

6 Psalm 139:7–12 MSG.

7 John 12:24–25.

8 Thomas Kelly, *A Testament of Devotion* (New York: Harper-Collins, 1969), 42.

9 St. John of the Cross, *The Dark Night of the Soul*, trans. and ed. E. Allison Peers (New York: Image Books/Doubleday, 2005).

10 Barbara Brown Taylor, *Learning to Walk in the Dark* (New York: HarperOne, 2014), 145.

11 John 15:1–5.

12 John 15:12–14.

13 Merton, *Dialogues with Silence*, 9.

14 Voskamp, *One Thousand Gifts*, 40.

CHAPTER TWELVE

1 George Eliot, *Middlemarch*, Project Gutenberg, http://www.gutenberg.org/files/145/145-h/145-h.htm.

2 Job 3:20–21.

3 Job 42:3.

4 Job 42:5.

5 Job 42:12.

6 Taylor, *Learning to Walk in the Dark*, 75.

7 Ibid.

8 Nouwen, *Life of the Beloved*, 77.

9 2 Corinthians 3:17–18.

10 Greg Boyd, *Seeing Is Believing: Experience Jesus through Imaginative Prayer* (Grand Rapids, MI: Baker Books, 2004), 79–80.

11 Foster, *Celebration of Discipline*, 26.

12 This story appears in John 8:2–11.

13 John Eldredge, *Waking the Dead: The Secret to a Heart Fully Alive* (Nashville: Thomas Nelson, 2016), 128.

14 Boyd, *Seeing Is Believing*, 88.

15 *Rooted Prayer* and *Rooted Listening* are courses designed and led by Roots&Branches Network, www.rootsandbranchesnetwork.com.

16 Quoted in Eldredge, *Waking the Dead*, 147.

17 Randy Clark, *Power to Heal* (Shippensburg, PA: Destiny Image, 2015), 81.

CHAPTER THIRTEEN

1 "Teresa Avila Quotes," The Order of Carmelites, https://ocarm.org/en/content/ocarm/teresa-avila-quotes.

2 Ephesians 1:7–10

3 Joe Wilkinson, "Scientists Peek into the Hidden World of Tree Roots," *ProArb*, June 24, 2014, http://proarbmagazine.com/scientists-peek-hidden-world-tree-roots.

4 Tolkien, *Fellowship of the Ring*, 150.

5 1 Corinthians 12:12.

6 William E. Flippin, Jr., "Ubuntu: Applying African Philosophy in Building Community," Huffington Post blog, February 5, 2012, https://www.huffingtonpost.com/reverend-william-e-flippin-jr/ub, untu-applying-africanp_b_1243904.html.

7 Desmond Tutu, "Desmond Tutu Peace Foundation: Mission and Philosophy," http://www.tutufoundationusa.org/
   desmond-tutu-peace-foundation.

8 John 12:4–5.

9 Ephesians 5:21.

10 Ephesians 4:34–36.

11 Martin Luther King, Jr., "Remaining Awake through a
    Great Revolution" (Sermon at Washington National Cathe-
    dral, 1968), The Martin Luther King., Jr., Research and
    Education Institute, https://kinginstitute.stanford.edu/
    king-papers/publications/knock-midnight-
    inspiration-great-sermons-reverend-martin-luther-king-
    jr-10.

12 Merton, *New Seeds of Contemplation*, 157.

13 John 17:20–23.

14 Dietrich Bonhoeffer, *Life Together: The Classic Exploration of
    Christian Community* (New York: HarperCollins, 1954), 98.

15 Fred Rogers, *The World according to Mister Rogers: Important
    Things to Remember* (New York: Hachette Books, 2003), 81.

16 Brown, *Daring Greatly*, 75.

17 Henri Nouwen, "Listening as Spiritual Hospitality,"
    Meditation: March 11, Henri Nouwen Society, https://
    henrinouwen.org/meditation/listening-spiritual-
    hospitality.

CHAPTER FOURTEEN

1 Rainer Maria Rilke, "I Believe in All That Has Never Yet Been Spoken," Mystery of Ascension, https://mysteryofascension.com/all-that-has-never-yet-been-spoken.

2 John 5:19.

3 John 15:8–11.

4 Andrew Murray, *Abiding in Christ*, 122.

5 John 15:12–17.

6 Nouwen, *You Are the Beloved*, 241.

7 This story appears in Luke 19:1–9.

8 Bob Goff, *Love Does: Discover a Secretly Incredible Life in an Ordinary World* (Nashville: Thomas Nelson, 2012), 129.

9 Ephesians 2:10, NRSV.

10 N. T. Wright, *A Whistle Stop Tour of Ephesians*, N. T. Wright Online, http://ntwrightonline.org/wp-content/uploads/2017/02/A-Whistle-Stop-Tour-of-Ephesians.pdf.

11 Revelation 22:1–2.

12 Saint Symeon the New Theologian, "Hymn 15: We Awaken in Christ's Body" from *The Enlightened Heart: An Anthology of Sacred Poetry*, ed. Stephen Mitchell (New York: Harper-Perennial, 1993), 38f.

ACKNOWLEDGMENTS

LIFE AND EVERY GOOD THING are born from connection. And my connections with these people have given life to me. This book and all it contains come from relationship with God, with family, with friends, with teachers and counselors and spiritual directors. I could not begin to name them all. But here are a few of the most important.

Dave, your love, encouragement, and steady commitment to my dreams and callings carry me. Doing life with you is a gift.

Jenny Jackson, Anya Carl-Heinbaugh, David Sheldon, Steve Eklund, Dana Cochran, Donna Painter, Jenny Phillips, and the whole Roots&Branches team—this book would not exist without you, your prophetic encouragement, and your passionate hearts. The best thing about this adventure is all of you.

Bob Kitson. You told me about Jesus. And that changed everything.

Deep River Books. Thank you, Bill Carmichael, for seeing the value in this message and giving this first-time author a chance. Thank you Andy Carmichael, Tamara Barnet, and the entire Deep River editorial team for helping to make this book so much more than I could have imagined.